Structure & Speaking Practice
Singapore

NATIONAL
GEOGRAPHIC
L E A R N I N G

Australia • Brazil • Mexico • Singapore • United Kingdom • United States

National Geographic Learning,
a Cengage Company

Structure & Speaking Practice, Singapore

Becky Tarver Chase

Publisher: Sherrise Roehr

Executive Editor: Laura LeDréan

Managing Editor: Jennifer Monaghan

Digital Implementation Manager,
Irene Boixareu

Senior Media Researcher: Leila Hishmeh

Director of Global Marketing: Ian Martin

Regional Sales and National Account
Manager: Andrew O'Shea

Content Project Manager: Ruth Moore

Senior Designer: Lisa Trager

Manufacturing Planner: Mary Beth
Hennebury

Composition: Lumina Datamatics

For permission to use material from this text or product,
submit all requests online at **cengage.com/permissions**
Further permissions questions can be emailed to
permissionrequest@cengage.com

Student Edition: Structure & Speaking Practice, Singapore
ISBN-13: 978-0-357-13798-7

National Geographic Learning
20 Channel Center Street
Boston, MA 02210
USA

Locate your local office at **international.cengage.com/region**

Visit National Geographic Learning online at **ELTNGL.com**
Visit our corporate website at **www.cengage.com**

Printed in China
Print Number: 02   Print Year: 2019

Photo credits

Scope and Sequence

ACADEMIC SKILLS

	Unit Title & Theme	Listenings & Video	Listening & Note Taking
1	**OUR ACTIVE EARTH** *page 1* ACADEMIC TRACK: Earth Science	**Lesson A** An Earth Science Lecture (with slide show) **VIDEO** Volcano Trek **Lesson B** A Discussion about Volcanoes	• Listening for Transitions • Using a Chart to Take Notes
2	**WONDERS FROM THE PAST** *page 21* ACADEMIC TRACK: Archaeology/Anthropology	**Lesson A** A Guided Tour of Uxmal **VIDEO** Sarah Parcak: Space Archaeologist and Egyptologist **Lesson B** A Conversation about an Assignment	• Listening for Examples • Recording Examples
3	**ENTREPRENEURS AND INNOVATORS** *page 41* ACADEMIC TRACK: Business	**Lesson A** A Presentation about a Success Story (with slide show) **VIDEO** Eco-Fuel Africa **Lesson B** A Conversation about Jack Andraka	• Distinguishing Facts and Opinions • Reviewing and Editing Your Notes

Speaking & Presentation	Vocabulary	Grammar & Pronunciation	Critical Thinking
• Using Transitions • Speaking at the Right Pace **Lesson Task** Interviewing a Partner about an Experience **Final Task** Giving a Presentation about a Natural Disaster	Using *Affect* and *Effect*	• Gerunds as Subjects and Objects • Syllable Number and Syllable Stress Review	**Focus** Predicting Exam Questions Analyzing, Applying, Evaluating, Interpreting a Diagram, Interpreting a Map, Making Inferences, Organizing Ideas, Prior Knowledge, Reflecting
• Summarizing • Using Index Cards **Lesson Task** Presenting Ancient Artifacts **Final Task** Giving a Presentation about a Historical Site	Using Antonyms	• The Passive Voice with the Past • Question Intonation	**Focus** Applying Knowledge Analyzing, Applying, Brainstorming, Evaluating, Making Inferences, Organizing Ideas, Prior Knowledge, Reflecting
• Rephrasing • Thinking about Your Audience **Lesson Task** Interpreting Quotations **Final Task** Presenting a New Product	Recognizing Adjectives and Adverbs	• The Present Perfect and Signal Words • Infinitives to Show Purpose • Thought Groups	**Focus** Interpreting Data Analyzing, Brainstorming, Interpreting Quotations, Organizing Ideas, Personalizing, Prior Knowledge, Ranking, Reflecting

Independent Student Handbook, p. 61   Vocabulary Index, p. 76

OUR ACTIVE EARTH

1

On June 15, 1991, Mount Pinatubo in the Philippines erupted, destroying everything in its path and killing 847 people.

ACADEMIC SKILLS

LISTENING Listening for Transitions
Using a Chart to Take Notes

SPEAKING Using Transitions

THINK AND DISCUSS

1 What's happening in the photo?

2 Can you name any other volcanoes? Where are they?

3 Look at the unit title. What are some topics you think

Look at the photo and the map. Then discuss these questions.

1. Have you ever heard of the San Andreas Fault? If so, what do you know about it?

2. What does the color red mean on this map?

3. In which places are earthquakes most likely to occur? Least likely?

4. What does the map show about your country?

THE WORLD'S EARTHQUAKE ZONES

The San Andreas Fault cuts across the Carrizo Plain in San Luis Obispo County, California, USA.

This map shows the world's earthquake zones, or areas of the world where earthquakes are most likely to occur.

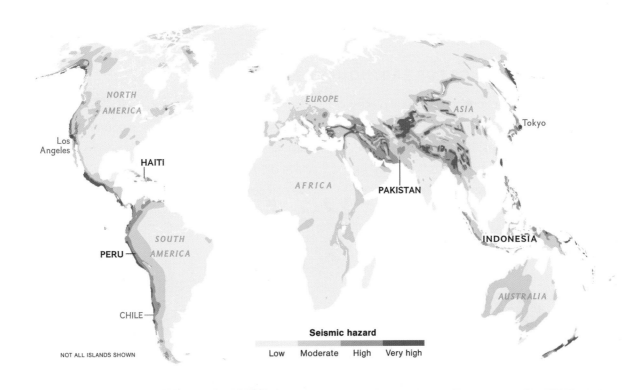

NORTH AMERICA

Los Angeles

HAITI

EUROPE

ASIA

Tokyo

AFRICA

PAKISTAN

INDONESIA

SOUTH AMERICA

PERU

AUSTRALIA

CHILE

NOT ALL ISLANDS SHOWN

Seismic hazard

Low   Moderate   High   Very high

A Vocabulary

INEXPENSIVE BUILDINGS FOR EARTHQUAKE ZONES

The earth's outer layer consists of several pieces called tectonic plates. The places where these plates meet are called **boundaries**. Tectonic plates are always moving. Sometimes the plates "jump" as they move. When this happens, **earthquakes** can occur.

Regions where earthquakes are more likely to occur are called earthquake **zones**. Some of the countries inside these zones are Pakistan, Haiti, Peru, and Indonesia. All of these countries have experienced **major** earthquakes, and many people have died because of unsafe buildings. Fortunately, we can **construct** inexpensive houses that will allow more people to **survive** earthquakes in developing parts of the world.

Pakistan

Light walls: Lightweight walls are less affected by earthquakes and are less likely to fall when the ground **shakes**. In Pakistan, a **material** called plaster is used to help **reinforce** the inside and outside of straw walls.

Haiti

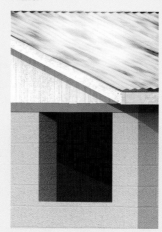

Light roofs: Metal roofs are lighter than concrete and won't **collapse** when an earthquake occurs.

Small windows: Small windows mean that walls are stronger.

Peru

Reinforced walls: Walls do not have to be reinforced with steel[1] or other kinds of metal. In Peru, plastic is sometimes used to reinforce walls.

Indonesia

Enclosed[2] materials: In Indonesia, concrete[3] and metal rods hold brick walls together so that in an earthquake, the whole wall moves as one piece.

[1]**steel** (n): strong, hard material [2]**enclosed** (v): to be inside or within something [3]**concrete** (n): a hard material made of sand, water, and cement

B Choose T for *True* or F for *False* for each statement. Correct the false statements. Use the context in exercise A to help you.

1. If a house or building collapses, it falls down.   T   F
2. When something shakes, it doesn't move.   T   F
3. If someone survives an earthquake, it means they are killed in it.   T   F
4. A boundary marks an area's limits.   T   F
5. When you construct something, you take it down.   T   F
6. Construction materials include concrete, metal, and bricks.   T   F
7. A zone is similar to an area.   T   F
8. We reinforce walls to make them weaker.   T   F
9. Major earthquakes are powerful and dangerous.   T   F
10. Earthquakes are caused by the movement of tectonic plates.   T   F

C Fill in each blank with the correct form of a word in **blue** from exercise A.

1. Buildings that _____ during an earthquake are dangerous. People can be killed or seriously injured when walls and roofs fall down.

2. It does not have to be expensive to _____ earthquake-safe houses. In Peru, for example, people use plastic to _____ walls and make them stronger.

3. You can protect your head by covering it with your arms during an earthquake. What are some other things you can do in order to _____ an earthquake?

4. When the earth _____, you can feel it. It's very scary!

5. In some places, people use natural _____ such as bamboo to make their walls stronger.

6. My country is in an earthquake _____, so I have experienced several earthquakes during my lifetime.

7. Occasionally earthquakes happen outside the _____ of earthquake zones. A rare earthquake in Washington, D.C., for instance, damaged the Washington Monument.

8. If you live in a(n) _____ zone, keep a bag of emergency supplies ready to go.

9. I've experienced a small earthquake but never a(n) _____ one, fortunately.

D Work in a group. Discuss these questions.

CRITICAL THINKING: ANALYZING

1. How does each house on page 4 keep people safe during an earthquake? Explain.
2. Which house on page 4 do you think would be the cheapest to construct? Explain.
3. Have you ever experienced an earthquake? If so, what happened?

A Listening An Earth Science Lecture

BEFORE LISTENING

CRITICAL THINKING:
INTERPRETING
A MAP

A Work with a partner. Look at the map and discuss the questions below.

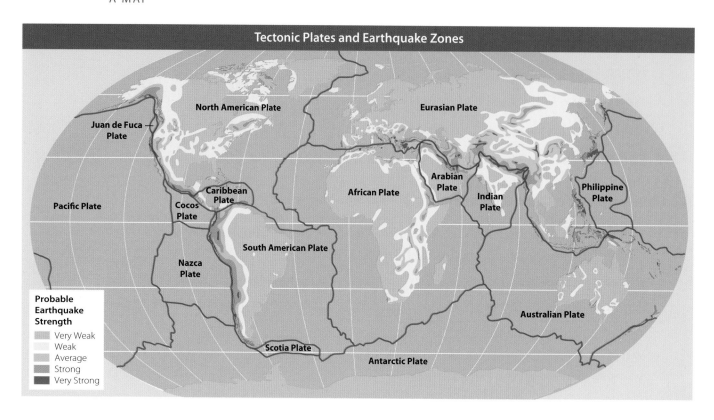

Tectonic Plates and Earthquake Zones

North American Plate

Juan de Fuca — Plate

Eurasian Plate

Pacific Plate

Caribbean Plate

Cocos Plate

African Plate

Arabian Plate

Indian Plate

Philippine Plate

South American Plate

Nazca Plate

Australian Plate

Probable Earthquake Strength
- Very Weak
- Weak
- Average
- Strong
- Very Strong

Scotia Plate

Antarctic Plate

1. What do the colors on this map represent?
2. What do you think the green lines on the map represent?
3. What are some areas of the world that have very strong earthquakes?

WHILE LISTENING

LISTENING FOR
MAIN IDEAS

B 🎧 Track 2 ▶ 1.1 Read the questions. Then listen to the lecture and write the answers.

1. What is the main topic of the lecture? _____

2. According to the speaker, what are *boundaries*? _____

3. How many types of boundaries are there? _____

4. How did buildings in Chile keep people safe during a 2010 earthquake?

_____

When you're listening to a lecture, it is sometimes helpful to use a chart to take notes. You can also use a chart after you listen to organize the information from your notes. As you review your notes, look for pieces of information that you can organize into categories. Using a chart to take and organize your notes will help you better understand and remember the most important information from the lecture.

C 🎧 **Track 2** Look at the chart. What information do you need in order to complete the chart? Listen again and take notes on the missing information.

NOTE TAKING

Types of Tectonic Boundaries

Boundary Type	Convergent		Transform
Movement	Plates come together; one plate can move under or over another.	Plates move apart.	
Results		A body of water can form between the two plates.	

AFTER LISTENING

CRITICAL THINKING Predicting Exam Questions

Predicting exam questions is a helpful technique for learning and remembering key ideas about a topic. As you review your notes and textbook, think about which information is the most important. That's the information that is most likely to be on an exam. Even if you are not studying for an exam, thinking about possible exam questions can help you succeed on other types of assignments.

D Look at the information from exercises A , B, and C. With a partner, think of at least five questions that might be on an exam and write them below. Some questions could be general, and others might be more specific.

CRITICAL THINKING: PREDICTING EXAM QUESTIONS

1. _____
2. _____
3. _____
4. _____
5. _____

E Form a group with another pair of students and take turns asking and answering each other's exam questions.

CRITICAL THINKING: ANALYZING

A Speaking

Transitions are words and phrases that show the relationship between ideas. Using transitions will help your listeners follow and understand your ideas more easily. Here are some examples of common transitions and how they are used:

To give additional information: *Furthermore, . . .*   *In addition, . . .*

> *These areas are places where earthquakes occur most often.* **Furthermore,** *the biggest, most dangerous earthquakes happen in these zones.*

To show contrast: *However, . . .*   *On the other hand, . . .*   *In contrast, . . .*

> *These houses—with lightweight walls and roofs—are still standing, and the people who live there are safe.* **In contrast,** *living in a part of the world where the buildings don't have these features can be quite dangerous.*

To give examples: *For example, . . .*   *For instance, . . .*

> *Buildings can be constructed with lighter materials.* **For instance,** *straw weighs much less than concrete.*

To talk about a result: *Therefore, . . .*   *As a result, . . .*

> *One plate can move under another plate.* **As a result,** *the mountains are pushed up even higher.*

A   Fill in each blank with an appropriate transition. Then work with a partner and compare your answers.

1. I didn't sleep much last night. _____, I'm very tired today.

2. The food at that restaurant isn't very good. _____, it's near my house, so I go there pretty often.

3. There are ways to help people after natural disasters. _____, you can donate money to humanitarian relief organizations.

4. That grocery store has a large selection of foods. _____, the prices are low, so we usually shop there.

5. This house is well constructed and big enough for our whole family. _____, it would be a safe place for all of us during an earthquake.

A woman in Aceh, Sumatra, Indonesia, walks on pieces of coral she brought into her house when it was flooded after an earthquake and a tsunami.

B Work with a partner. Take turns completing each statement with your own ideas.

1. We (do / don't) live in an earthquake zone. Therefore, . . .
2. We sometimes experience extreme weather here. For instance, . . .
3. I keep important papers in a backpack in case I need to leave the house suddenly during an emergency. Furthermore, . . .
4. I don't worry very much about earthquakes. On the other hand, . . .
5. After an earthquake, you may not be able to use your cell phone. In addition, . . .
6. California had dangerously high temperatures in 2015. As a result, . . .

GRAMMAR FOR SPEAKING Gerunds as Subjects and Objects

A *gerund* is the base form of a verb plus *-ing*. Gerunds act as nouns. We often use them as the subjects of sentences. Notice that a gerund subject is always singular.

> **Walking** *is my favorite form of exercise.*
> **Using** *lightweight materials for houses helps keep people safe.*

We also use gerunds as the objects of verbs or prepositions.

> *Today we're going to* <u>continue</u> **talking** *about plate tectonics.*
> *Lisa is interested* <u>in</u> **studying** *geology.*

Verbs that are often followed by a gerund object include:

admit	consider	dislike	finish	(don't) mind	postpone	suggest
avoid	discuss	enjoy	keep	miss	recommend	

C Fill in each blank with the gerund form of the verb in parentheses.

1. _____ (predict) an earthquake is not possible, unfortunately.

2. I never worry about _____ (be) killed in an earthquake. I don't live in an earthquake zone.

3. They suggest _____ (go) outside as soon as you feel an earthquake.

4. _____ (have) an earthquake safety plan is important for people in earthquake zones.

5. Sorry, would you mind _____ (repeat) that? I wasn't paying attention.

6. Are you interested in _____ (get) a degree in geology?

D Work with your partner. Take turns interviewing each other using the questions below. Practice using gerunds. Take notes on your partner's answers.

1. What are some things you enjoy doing in your free time? Why?
2. What are some things you are considering doing in the future? Why?
3. What are some things you dislike doing on the weekends? Why?

CRITICAL THINKING: **E** Form a group with another pair of students. Take turns telling the group about your
APPLYING partner. Use your notes from exercise D to help you. Practice using gerunds.

LESSON TASK Interviewing a Partner about an Experience

A 🎧 **Track 3** Look at the photo, and read the caption and information in the box on page 11. Then listen to information about a photographer and complete the sentences on page 11 with the gerunds you hear.

▶ **Surfers at Kirikiri Beach in Otsuchi-cho, Japan stand near a protective wall that was destroyed in the 2011 tsunami. In 2016, photographer Alejandro Chaskielberg took photos of places damaged by Japan's 2011 tsunami.**

On March 11, 2011, a strong earthquake under the Pacific Ocean caused a *tsunami*—a powerful ocean wave that moved onshore over a large area of Japan's eastern coast. The tsunami destroyed buildings and vehicles and caused major damage to a nuclear power plant. It also killed more than 16,000 people and injured many others.

Sadly, the death and destruction following a major natural disaster are not quickly forgotten. This story focuses on a photographer from Argentina and what he did to help the people of Japan.

1. _____ in Japan means _____ a lot about earthquakes.

2. Today, some Japanese people avoid _____ about the horror and sadness of the tsunami of 2011.

3. A photographer from Argentina went to Japan in 2016 with the goal of _____ survivors think about the tsunami in new ways.

4. _____ around the world is nothing new to Alejandro Chaskielberg.

5. He asked people to consider _____ to the places they lived or the places they went before the tsunami.

6. According to Chaskielberg, _____ these photos was ". . . a way to help them create new memories."

B Work with a partner. Discuss these questions. Use gerunds and transitions when appropriate.

CRITICAL THINKING: ANALYZING

1. Living anywhere in the world involves some kind of danger, from tsunamis and earthquakes to crime or dangerous roads. What are some of the dangers of living in your country?
2. Look at the photo on page 10. Why do you think Chaskielberg decided to take a photo of these people?
3. Why do you think Chaskielberg decided to go to a place damaged by the tsunami to take this picture? What questions do you think he asked the people in the photo?

C Work with a different partner. Interview your partner about a difficult experience in his or her life. In your notebook, take brief notes on the answers. Then switch roles and repeat.

1. What difficult event have you experienced? What happened? What did you do?
2. How did this experience affect you afterwards?
3. (your own question) _____

D Form a group with another pair of students. Tell the group about your partner's experience. Use your notes from exercise C to help you.

CRITICAL THINKING: APPLYING

Video

A climber stands above the lava lake inside the Erta Ale volcano in Ethiopia.

Volcano Trek

BEFORE VIEWING

A Look at the diagram below. Use the words from the diagram to complete the paragraph.

A VOLCANIC ERUPTION

A volcano is a mountain with a large hole at the top. This hole is called a(n) _____. A volcano produces very hot, melted rock. When it is underground, this hot, melted rock is called _____. When it leaves or comes out of the volcano, it is called _____. When the lava stays in the crater, it forms a(n) _____. When lava leaves a volcano, we say the volcano erupts. We call it a(n) _____.

1
2
3
4
5

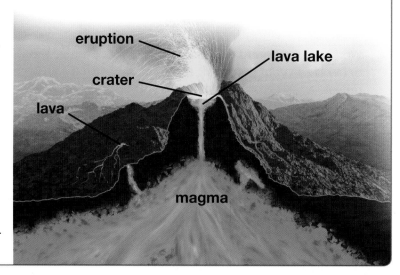

eruption

lava lake

crater

lava

magma

B Read the information about Dr. Franck Tessier and Dr. Irene Margaritis. With a partner, discuss what you know about volcanoes. Are there volcanoes in your country? Are they popular places to visit?

PRIOR KNOWLEDGE

> **MEET DR. FRANCK TESSIER AND DR. IRENE MARGARITIS.** They're National Geographic Explorers, geologists, and professors. They've traveled from France to Ethiopia to study a very unusual volcano: Erta Ale. It has the world's oldest lava lake, which is also one of the lowest points on Earth. Collecting and analyzing samples of the material in the lava lake could help the scientists learn more about the earth's beginnings.

WHILE VIEWING

C ▶ 1.2 Read the statements. Then watch the video and choose T for *True* and F for *False*. Correct the false statements.

UNDERSTANDING DETAILS

1. The temperature of the lava is more than 2,000° F.   T   F
2. The team uses horses to help them reach the lava lake.   T   F
3. The geologists are from the University of Paris.   T   F
4. Erta Ale is in the Afar area of Ethiopia.   T   F
5. As lava cools, it becomes red in color.   T   F
6. The team returns from the crater at 1:00 a.m.   T   F

D ▶ 1.2 Watch the video again and take notes on the information you see or hear that helps you answer this question: Do Dr. Franck Tessier and Dr. Irene Margaritis enjoy their work as geologists?

CRITICAL THINKING: MAKING INFERENCES

_____

_____

AFTER VIEWING

E Write two questions you'd like to ask the geologists in the video.

_____

_____

F Work in a group. Share your questions from exercise E.

Vocabulary

A 🎧 **Track 4** Read and listen to the information. Notice each word or phrase in **blue** and think about its meaning.

> ### THE PACIFIC RING OF FIRE: FAST FACTS
>
> 1. The Ring of Fire consists of many volcanoes in a near-circle around the Pacific Ocean.
> 2. **Active** volcanoes are dangerous. People choose to live near them, however, because volcanic **soil** is rich and good for farming.
> 3. In Indonesia, more people live near active volcanoes than in any other country. On the island of Java alone, there are more than 30 volcanoes and about 140 million people.
> 4. One of the world's worst natural **disasters** occurred in Indonesia in 1883. The **eruption** of Mount Krakatau, a volcanic island near Java, caused a tsunami that killed more than 36,000 people. In addition, it produced enough volcanic ash[1] to **affect** the earth's weather for several months.
>
>
>
> **An aerial view of Mount Tavurvur, an active volcano in Rabaul, Papua New Guinea**
>
> 5. In Kinarejo, Java, many farmers live near a volcano called Mount Merapi. A man there named Mbah Marijan was known as the "Gatekeeper of Merapi." **According to** tradition, the Gatekeeper knew the volcano very well, and his job was to tell people when it became dangerous so that they could **evacuate**. Sadly, Marijan and many others were killed when Mount Merapi erupted violently in 2010.
> 6. For people who live near volcanoes, evacuating means **leaving behind** their homes, animals, and daily lives. Therefore, they often wait for **definite** news about the volcano that will **justify** their leaving. However, sometimes the news doesn't come in time to save lives.

[1]**ash** (n): burnt material

B Match each word or phrase from exercise A with its definition.

1. _____ active (adj)
2. _____ soil (n)
3. _____ disasters (n)
4. _____ eruption (n)
5. _____ affect (v)
6. _____ according to (prep)
7. _____ evacuate (v)
8. _____ leaving behind (v)
9. _____ definite (adj)
10. _____ justify (v)

a. unlikely to be changed
b. things that have very bad effects or results
c. to make right or necessary
d. phrase that tells us where information comes from
e. to leave an area because of some danger
f. not taking something with you when you leave
g. a sudden explosion of rocks, ash, and lava
h. the material on the earth's surface in which plants grow
i. with volcanoes, having recently erupted or likely to erupt
j. to influence or change something

C Complete each sentence with two or more words. Use your own ideas. Then work with a partner and take turns saying your sentences.

1. Volcanic eruptions are dangerous because _____.

2. According to my parents, _____.

3. If we ever need to evacuate this building, I'll _____.

4. The worst natural disaster that I remember was _____.

5. Active volcanoes are _____.

6. _____ affects my life every day.

VOCABULARY SKILL Using *Affect* and *Effect*

It's easy to confuse the words *affect* and *effect* since they look and sound so similar. However, *affect* almost always acts as a verb, and *effect* almost always acts as a noun.

verb: *Sunshine **affects** the way I feel.*
noun: *Sunshine has a positive **effect** on my mood.*

D Choose the correct word to complete each sentence.

1. Natural disasters in the Ring of Fire (affect / effect) a large number of people.
2. What are the (affects / effects) of a major earthquake?
3. A major hurricane actually (affects / effects) ocean life in the area.
4. Volcanic eruptions have a positive (affect / effect) on the soil.
5. How did seeing those photos of the earthquake (affect / effect) you?
6. Fortunately, the storm didn't (affect / effect) our area.
7. The documentary showed the (affects / effects) of the 2015 earthquake in Nepal.
8. Volcanic ash can have an (affect / effect) on the weather.

Listening A Discussion about Volcanoes

BEFORE LISTENING

PREDICTING **A** You are going to listen to a group of students discussing volcanoes during a study session for an Earth Science class. Discuss this question with a partner: What topics related to volcanoes do you think the students will discuss, (e.g., the dangers of volcanoes, magma and lava)?

WHILE LISTENING

LISTENING FOR
MAIN IDEAS
B 🎧 **Track 5** Listen to the discussion. Choose the three topics the speakers discuss. Did they mention any of the topics you discussed in exercise A?

    a. the material inside volcanos

    b. why volcanos are dangerous to people

    c. how to tell when a volcano will erupt soon

    d. the Gatekeeper in Indonesia

    e. the number of people killed when Mount Merapi erupted

C 🎧 **Track 5** Listen again and complete each sentence with the information you hear.

LISTENING FOR
DETAILS

1. When melted rock is _____ the earth, it's called magma.

2. When it comes *out* of the earth, it's called _____ .

3. According to Professor Lopez, lava can kill people and _____ .

4. U.S. government geologists told everyone to _____ before Mount Saint Helens erupted.

5. _____ people were killed when Mount Saint Helens erupted.

6. The Gatekeeper is an important part of village _____ .

Mount Nyiragongo, Democratic Republic of the Congo

It's important to listen for transitions in speech so that you have an idea of what the speaker is going to say next.

Remember, if you hear *in addition* and *furthemore*, the speaker is going to provide more information.

> *There will be two exams this semester.* **In addition,** *we'll have three quizzes.*

When you hear *in contrast, however,* or *on the other hand,* the speaker is going to talk about a contrast or an exception.

> *Living near volcanoes isn't always safe.* **However,** *the land near volcanoes is excellent for farming.*

When you hear *for example* or *for instance,* the speaker is going to provide an example.

> *There are other ways to communicate.* **For example,** *you can mail a letter if you don't have an Internet connection.*

When you hear *therefore* or *as a result,* the speaker is going to talk about a result.

> *The prime minister has a serious illness.* **Therefore,** *she has canceled the trip.*

D 🎧 **Track 6** Work with a partner. Discuss these excerpts from the conversation. Which kind of transition do you think each speaker used? Complete each excerpt with a transition. Then listen and check your answers.

LISTENING FOR
TRANSITIONS

1. **Khaled:** Professor Lopez said that when there's an eruption, hot lava can kill people

   and start fires. _____, he talked about huge rocks and hardened lava. I

1

   wouldn't want to be nearby when those fly out!

   Tony: Me neither! _____, all of that stuff from inside volcanoes

2

   makes good soil eventually.

2. **Ann:** … Personally, I'd rather get my volcano news from scientists. After all,

   it was geologists working for the U.S. government who told everyone in the area

   to evacuate before Mount Saint Helens erupted. … Some people stayed, and

   _____, 57 people were killed when the volcano erupted.

3

AFTER LISTENING

E Work with a partner. Discuss these questions.

CRITICAL THINKING:
REFLECTING

1. Do you think the study group was helpful for the students? Why or why not?
2. Have you ever seen a volcano? If so, describe it. If not, would you like to? Why or why not?

B Speaking

A 🎧 **Track 8** Work with a partner. Say each word aloud. Underline the stressed syllable in each word. Then count the number of syllables in each word and write it on the line. Listen and check your answers.

1. common _____
2. practical _____
3. circumstances _____
4. flow _____
5. summarize _____

6. clothes _____
7. psychological _____
8. recommend _____
9. reinforce _____
10. definitely _____

B Work with a partner. Say either option *a* or *b* for each item below. Your partner will listen and tell you which one you said. Then switch roles and repeat.

A: *You can turn it.*
B: *You said b.*
A: *That's right!*

1. a. You can return it.
2. a. We demand it.
3. a. common
4. a. It's likely.
5. a. definite
6. a. We need a research team.

b. You can turn it.
b. We demanded it.
b. Come in.
b. It's unlikely.
b. Define it.
b. We need a search team.

FINAL TASK Giving a Presentation about a Natural Disaster

> You are going to give an individual presentation about a natural disaster. You will choose a natural disaster and present it to the class.

A Work with a partner. Discuss whether you think each statement in the quiz is true or false. Choose T for *True* or F for *False* for each statement. Use expressions from the Everyday Language box when necessary. Then check your answers below.

CRITICAL THINKING: EVALUATING

QUIZ: WHAT DO YOU KNOW ABOUT NATURAL DISASTERS?

1. A tornado can produce the fastest winds of any storm on Earth. T F

2. An avalanche can be caused by the movement of tectonic plates. T F

3. The strongest earthquake in history occurred in Indonesia. T F

4. Your chances of being hit by lightning in a given year are 1 in 7,000. T F

5. An island near Long Island was completely destroyed by a hurricane. T F

6. Landslides can hit any country with steep mountains and heavy rain. T F

7. One forest fire in the United States killed more than 1,700 people. T F

8. Tiny particles of frozen water fall from the sky during ice storms. T F

EVERYDAY LANGUAGE Making Guesses

It could be …   *It's probably …*   *It might be …*   *I guess …*   *I think …*

Answers: **1.** T (up to 300 mph/500 kph) **2.** T **3.** F (in Chile in 1960) **4.** F (1 in 700,000) **5.** T (Hog Island in 1893) **6.** T **7.** T (the Peshtigo Fire in 1871) **8.** F (cold liquid raindrops freeze as soon as they touch a surface)

Trees and a car covered in ice in Versoix, on the shore of Lake Geneva, Switzerland

B Work in a group. Discuss the natural disasters below. What do you know about them? Which topic is the most interesting to you? Explain.

avalanche	flood	heat wave	ice storm	tornado
drought	forest fire	hurricane	landslide	tsunami

C Work on your own. Choose one of the natural disasters from exercise B as the topic for your presentation. Do some research to learn about your topic. You can use the Internet, an encyclopedia, information from this book, or interview someone you know to get information.

D Use the questions below to help you organize the information about your topic. In your notebook, write brief notes to answer each question. Then think about which transitions might be helpful to connect your ideas.

1. Where and when does this kind of natural disaster usually occur (e.g., in cold places, warm places, during certain times of the year)?
2. What are the causes of this kind of natural disaster?
3. What happens when this kind of disaster occurs?
4. What are some things people should or shouldn't do when this natural disaster occurs?

> **PRESENTATION SKILL** Speaking at the Right Pace
>
> Many people get nervous and speak too quickly when they give a presentation. When you do this, your audience might not understand everything you are saying. When you give a presentation, it's important to remember to slow down and pause occasionally so that your audience has time to think about what you are saying.
>
> It's also important not to speak too slowly. This can make your speech sound unnatural. It's OK to slow down occasionally to emphasize an important idea, but in general, try to find the right pace for speaking to an audience—not too fast and not too slow.

E Present your topic to the class. Remember to speak at the right pace. Use transition words and phrases when necessary.

REFLECTION

1. What are two ways that predicting exam questions might be useful to you?

_____

_____

2. What events from your life did the topic of natural disasters make you remember or think about?

_____

_____

3. Here are the vocabulary words and phrases from the unit. Check (✓) the ones you can use.

☐ according to	☐ disaster	☐ material
☐ active	☐ earthquake	☐ reinforce AWL
☐ affect AWL	☐ eruption	☐ shake
☐ boundary	☐ evacuate	☐ soil
☐ collapse AWL	☐ justify AWL	☐ survive AWL
☐ construct AWL	☐ leave behind	☐ zone
☐ definite AWL	☐ major AWL	

WONDERS FROM THE PAST 2

An ancient Moai statue
on Easter Island

CLUES TO THE PAST

EXPLORE THE THEME

Look at the photos and read the information. Then discuss these questions.

1. Which of the ancient civilizations mentioned on these pages have you heard of? What do you know about them?

2. Which of the artifacts on these pages do you find most interesting? Why?

3. What kinds of "clues" or information do you think the artifacts on these pages can give us about the ancient civilizations they come from?

4. What other ancient civilizations do you know about? What do you know about them?

What was daily life like for the ancient Egyptians, the ancient Greeks, or the Maya? What did they eat and drink? How did they dress and spend their free time? These are some of the questions that archaeologists try to answer through their work. And although we may never have all of the answers, the artifacts left behind by these ancient civilizations provide some clues to what life may have been like for people hundreds and thousands of years ago.

A decorated container from the Maya civilization, Mexico

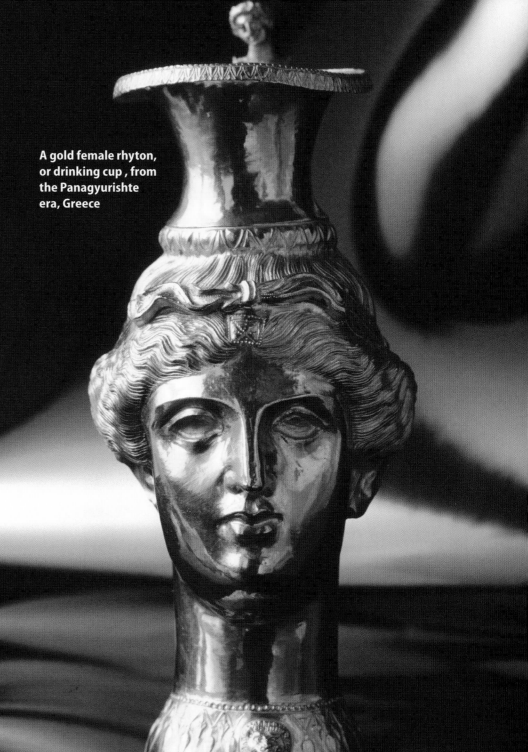

A gold female rhyton, or drinking cup , from the Panagyurishte era, Greece

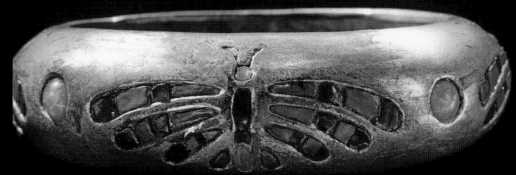

A gold bracelet that was discovered in the burial chamber of Egyptian Queen Hetepheres, mother of Cheops, of the IV Dynasty, Egypt

A Vocabulary

MEANING FROM CONTEXT

A 🎧 **Track 9** Look at the images, and read and listen to the information. Notice each word in **blue** and think about its meaning.

AN AMAZING DISCOVERY

Every career has a high point, and according to National Geographic Explorer William Saturno, being the first human being in 2,000 years to view a beautiful Maya mural[1] in Guatemala was probably that point for him. Saturno, an **archaeologist** and an expert on the Maya **civilization**, discovered the mural inside a room that was once next to a pyramid[2]. The mural room and pyramid were later covered by a larger pyramid—part of the **ruins** of an **ancient** Maya city, now called San Bartolo.

At first, Saturno could see only a small part of the mural. He had to **dig** through earth and stone in order to **reveal** the rest. Then, instead of using a camera, Saturno used his scanner[3] to take digital **images** of the mural. He took about 350 scans!

The mural wasn't the only important find at San Bartolo. The archaeologists also uncovered a **tomb**. It was a **royal** tomb, where the bones of a Maya king were **buried**, along with objects such as a bowl in the shape of a frog and an image of the Maya rain god Chac.

[1]**mural** (n): a picture painted on a wall
[2]**pyramid** (n): a huge building used as a tomb or ceremonial site
[3]**scanner** (n): a device that "reads" an image and changes it to digital information

B Write each word in blue from exercise A next to its definition.

1. _____ (n) a place that contains the body of a dead person

2. _____ (n) pictures

3. _____ (v) to use the hands or a tool to make a hole in the ground

4. _____ (v) put into the ground and covered with earth or stone

5. _____ (n) a person who studies the past by uncovering ancient sites and objects

6. _____ (adj) having to do with kings, queens, princes, or their families

7. _____ (adj) extremely old

8. _____ (n) broken parts of buildings that still exist after a long time

9. _____ (v) to show or uncover something so that people can see it

10. _____ (n) a human society with a complex social organization

C Work with a partner. Take turns asking and answering these questions.

CRITICAL THINKING: REFLECTING

1. Where in the world can you see pyramids?
2. What ancient cultures have you studied? What do you remember about them?
3. What famous archaeological site would you like to visit? Why?
4. What kinds of things do archaeologists dig for? What do they hope to find?
5. What ancient civilizations are there in your part of the world?

VOCABULARY SKILL Using Antonyms

An *antonym* is a word that means the opposite of another word. Learning antonyms can help you build your vocabulary and better express your ideas.

| *ancient / modern* | *reveal / hide* | *buried / uncovered* |

D Work with a partner. Discuss the meaning of the underlined word in each statement. Then match the correct antonym with each underlined word.

Antonyms

1. _____ In years with enough rain, food was <u>abundant</u>.   a. similar

2. _____ The Great Pyramid at Giza is <u>enormous</u>, rising more than 450 feet into the air.   b. scarce

3. _____ We have some <u>general</u> ideas about the ruins, but few details.   c. tiny

4. _____ The Egyptian pyramids all have the same shape, but the Pyramid of the Magician in Mexico is <u>distinct</u>.   d. specific

5. _____ Before people lived in cities, human societies had a <u>simple</u> structure: Adults either hunted animals or gathered plants for food.   e. complex

A Listening A Guided Tour of Uxmal

BEFORE LISTENING

PRIOR KNOWLEDGE **A** Work with a partner. Discuss these questions.

1. Where did the ancient Maya people live?
2. What do you know about the Maya? For example, did they live in cities?

WHILE LISTENING

LISTENING FOR MAIN IDEAS **B** 🎧 **Track 10** Listen to the guided tour. Choose the correct answer to each question.

1. Which Maya site are the tourists visiting?

   a. Tulum
   b. Palenque
   c. Uxmal

2. Why is this one of the most popular Maya historical sites?

   a. It has several pyramids and other structures.
   b. It has a ball court.
   c. It's easy to get to.

3. Why is the Pyramid of the Magician unusual?

   a. It has rounded sides.
   b. It has triangular sides.
   c. It has flat sides.

The Pyramid of the Magician and the ball court at Uxmal, Yucatán, Mexico

The stone goal ring from the ball court at Uxmal, Yucatán, Mexico

C 🎧 **Track 10** Listen again and write notes to answer the questions.

LISTENING FOR
DETAILS

1. From which period of Maya history is this site? _____

2. According to an old story, how long did it take to build the Pyramid of the Magician?

   _____

3. Around how many years did it actually take to build the pyramid? _____

4. How many different structures make up the pyramid? _____

5. Where does the group go after seeing the pyramid? _____

6. What is in front of the Governor's Palace? _____

7. What is a *jaguar*? _____

AFTER LISTENING

D Work with a partner. Imagine that you are going to speak to the tour guide at Uxmal. Write three questions about the Maya civilization to ask him. These questions can be about any part of Maya life (e.g., food, clothing, housing).

1. _____?

2. _____?

3. _____?

E Form a group with another pair of students. Share your questions from exercise D. Explain why you want to know the answers to your questions.

A Speaking

PRONUNCIATION Question Intonation

🎧 **Track 11** Intonation can help people understand the kind of question you are asking.

1. In *yes/no* questions, the speaker's voice usually rises at the end of the question.

   Is the Maya ball game still played here?

2. In questions that offer choices, the speaker's voice rises for each option except the last one, where the speaker's voice falls.

   Would you rather leave now or later?

3. In *wh-* questions, the speaker's voice rises on the stressed syllable of the last content word and then falls at the end.

   *When was Uxmal **discovered**?*

A 🎧 **Track 12** Listen and draw rising or falling arrows according to the intonation you hear.

1. What time are we leaving?

2. Have you ever been to Kazakhstan?

3. How was the walking tour?

4. Did you go there on Friday or Saturday?

5. Is the mural from the early, middle, or late period?

6. Does this story make sense to you?

7. Is the mural in Mexico, Guatemala, or Honduras?

8. Where's the pyramid?

B Work with a partner. Compare your answers from exercise A. Then practice asking and answering the questions using the correct question intonation.

C With your partner, think of new questions to ask each other using the question words in the box.

Are...?	Is...?	Do...?	Does...?	Which...?
Why...?	Where...?	When...?	How many...?	Who...?

A: *Are you going to have lunch after class?*
B: *No, I have another class at 1:30.*

We form the passive voice in the past with *was/were* and the past participle of a verb.

*The walking tour **was given** by an archaeologist yesterday.*

Notice how questions are formed in the passive voice with the past.

***Were** a lot of people **buried** in the tombs?*

We use *by* with the passive when we want to specify who or what did the action. We generally use the passive voice without the *by* phrase when:

1. the agent (the "do-er") of an action is not known or not very important.

*The Pyramid of the Magician definitely **wasn't built** in one night.*

2. the agent is clear from the context.

*Corn **was grown** near the city of Uxmal.*

D Read the information about the Seven Wonders of the Ancient World. Then complete each sentence below using the passive with the past form of the verb in parentheses.

> The Seven Wonders of the Ancient World were remarkable structures in the Mediterranean region. They were listed in tourist guidebooks around 2,000 years ago. Today, the Great Pyramid at Giza in Egypt is the only "wonder" that is still standing.

1. The Temple of Artemis at Ephesus _____ (build) to honor a Greek goddess.

2. The Hanging Gardens of Babylon _____ (plant) by King Nebuchadnezzar II.

3. The Lighthouse of Alexandria _____ (construct) in the third century BC.

4. The Colossus of Rhodes _____ (destroy) by an earthquake.

5. The Statue of Zeus at Olympia _____ (keep) inside its own temple.

6. About eight hundred tons of stone _____ (need) every day to build the Great Pyramid at Giza.

7. The Mausoleum at Halicarnassus _____ (design) by Greek architects.

A man leads camels in the desert near the pyramids at Giza in Egypt.

29

CRITICAL THINKING:
APPLYING
KNOWLEDGE

E Work in a group. Compare your answers from exercise D. Then discuss these questions.

1. The Colossus of Rhodes and the Statue of Zeus at Olympia were large statues. What are other large statues you know about? Why do you think those statues were built?
2. The Hanging Gardens of Babylon are the only "living wonder." Why do you think the gardens were planted? What are some similar places that exist today? What do you know about them?
3. The Lighthouse of Alexandria may be the only wonder with an everyday purpose. Why do you think it was built?
4. The Great Pyramid at Giza and the Mausoleum at Halicarnassus were built to serve as tombs for important leaders. How are important leaders in your culture honored when they die?

LESSON TASK Presenting Ancient Artifacts

CRITICAL THINKING:
ANALYZING

A Work in a group of three. Look at the photos and read the captions on this page and the next about three ancient artifacts. Discuss these questions about each artifact.

1. Where was the artifact found?
2. When was it made?
3. What material was it made from?
4. What do you think it was used for?

1.

▲ This artifact is from the Anasazi civilization. It is either a spoon or a shovel made from the horn of an animal. The Anasazi lived in the southwestern United States, where this artifact was found.

2.

▲ This Maya mask was found in Mexico. It was the death mask of a Maya king named Pakal. It's made of jade, which is a smooth green stone.

3.

▲ This necklace was found on the Island of Crete, Greece. It was buried with a woman from ancient Greece. It's made of glass and gold.

EVERYDAY LANGUAGE   Expressing Certainty and Uncertainty

More certain:	Less certain:
I'm fairly sure…	*I'm not really sure…*
I'm almost positive…	*I'm not positive…*
I'm certain…	*I don't know…*

> *I'm certain this artifact was made from the horn of an animal, but I don't know what kind of animal the horn came from.*

B With your group, prepare a short presentation about the artifacts from exercise A. Write notes on your ideas in your notebook. Your presentation should include the following: ORGANIZING IDEAS

1. information that answers the questions from exercise A
2. some additional details from your own ideas. Use your imagination. (What words describe the artifact? Who do you think found it? What other artifacts do you think were found with it?)

C Practice your presentation with your group. Each student in your group should present one artifact.

D Get together with another group. Take turns presenting your artifacts.   PRESENTING

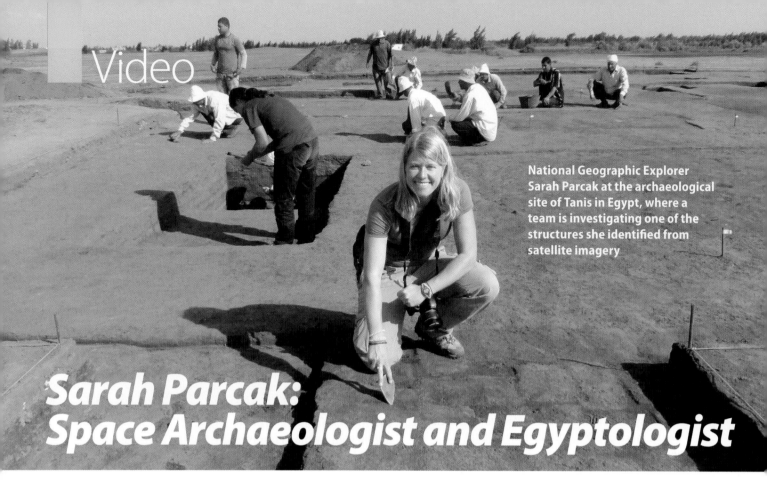

Video

National Geographic Explorer Sarah Parcak at the archaeological site of Tanis in Egypt, where a team is investigating one of the structures she identified from satellite imagery

Sarah Parcak:
Space Archaeologist and Egyptologist

BEFORE VIEWING

A Match each word or phrase from the video with its meaning. You may use a dictionary.

1. _____ archaeology
2. _____ satellite images
3. _____ excavate

4. _____ Egyptologist
5. _____ curiosity
6. _____ settlement

a. photos taken from a satellite in space
b. interest in knowing about things
c. the study of human history and pre-history and the materials and remains of ancient civilizations
d. to remove soil carefully in order to uncover things
e. a person who studies ancient Egypt
f. a place where a group of people live

B Work with a partner. Which of these facts about archaeology and space archaeology did you already know? Which fact is the most surprising to you? Explain.

1. Archaeologists spend a lot of their time working outdoors.
2. Space satellites can take pictures of what is under the earth's soil.
3. Archaeology helps us learn about people and civilizations of the past.

CRITICAL THINKING: MAKING INFERENCES

C Read the information about Sarah Parcak on the next page. With a partner, discuss how you think she feels about her job and why you think so.

MEET SARAH PARCAK. She's a National Geographic Explorer, a Space Archaeologist, and an Egyptologist. She's been interested in ancient history since childhood. She describes the moment she first saw the Great Pyramids of Egypt as "magical." These days, Parcak directs the Laboratory for Global Observation at the University of Alabama in the United States. There, she analyzes satellite images in order to locate ancient archaeological sites.

WHILE VIEWING

D ▶ 2.1 Watch the video and choose the correct answers.

UNDERSTANDING MAIN IDEAS

1. What does Sarah Parcak say is the most important thing about being an explorer?

   a. getting the necessary education in archaeology
   b. doing research on computers and smartphones
   c. being outside and looking at the world around us

2. What does Parcak say about her philosophy of archaeology?

   a. It's about finding gold jewelry and other treasures.
   b. It's about asking questions in order to understand the past.
   c. It's about understanding how the environment affected ancient people.

3. According to Parcak, what does archaeology help us understand?

   a. who we are and why we're here
   b. how to keep our past knowledge
   c. why life today is better than in the past

E ▶ 2.1 Read the statements. Then watch the video again and choose T for *True* or F for *False*. Correct the false statements.

UNDERSTANDING DETAILS

1. Parcak grew up doing activities outside, including camping and hiking.	T	F
2. She says curiosity motivates us to explore the world.	T	F
3. Parcak uses satellites to look into outer space.	T	F
4. She uses information that works like a space-based X-ray to see beneath the soil.	T	F
5. She has found more than 4,000 ancient settlements in Egypt.	T	F
6. Parcak can point to a single moment when she decided to be an archaeologist.	T	F

AFTER VIEWING

F Discuss these questions with a partner.

CRITICAL THINKING: REFLECTING

1. Do you enjoy being outdoors and exploring the world? Explain.
2. What are two questions you would like to ask Sarah Parcak?

B Vocabulary

A 🎧 **Track 13** Read and listen to the information. Notice each word in **blue** and think about its meaning.

NEW CLUES ABOUT TUTANKHAMEN: HIS LIFE AND DEATH

In 1922, British Egyptologist Howard Carter found the **remains** of a young man in a tomb filled with royal **treasures** in the Valley of the Kings, Egypt. Newspapers around the world **reported** the **discovery** and described the gold jewelry, **precious** stones, and beautiful art found in the tomb. Everyone wanted to know who this important man was.

We now know Tutankhamen was the son of Akhenaten, and he **ruled** Egypt from 1332–1322 BC. He became pharaoh[1] as a child, and he died young. Yet many questions are still unanswered. Was "Tut" ill? Was he murdered[2]? What did he look like when he was **alive**?

In 2005, scientists began to **analyze** Tut's remains with computer tomography (CT) and modern forensic medicine—a science usually used to **investigate** and solve murder cases. Tut's remains were scanned in a CT machine, which created 3-D images. Using this technology, scientists **determined** that Tut was probably not murdered and was about 19 when he died.

Scientists also worked with an artist to construct a life-like model of Tut. Not everyone likes the result, but according to the CT scans, he probably looked a lot like modern Egyptians.

[1]**pharoah** (n): a ruler or king of ancient Egypt
[2]be **murdered** (v): to be killed by someone

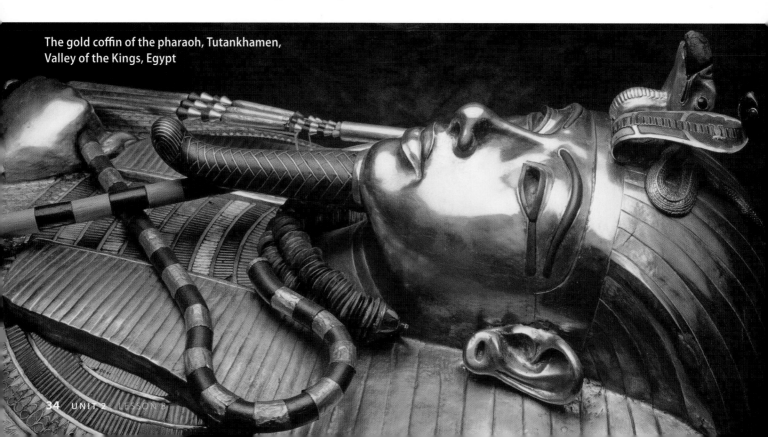

The gold coffin of the pharaoh, Tutankhamen, Valley of the Kings, Egypt

B Write each word in **blue** from exercise A next to its definition.

1. _____ (n) valuable objects

2. _____ (v) to look at something carefully in order to understand it

3. _____ (adj) very valuable

4. _____ (n) the finding of something new

5. _____ (v) told about something (e.g., an event)

6. _____ (adj) living, not dead

7. _____ (v) controlled (e.g., a country)

8. _____ (v) to search for facts and information

9. _____ (n) parts or things that are left after death or destruction

10. _____ (v) concluded or decided

C Complete each sentence with the correct form of a word from exercise B.

1. She's a statistician. She _____ numerical data.

2. Our country's most important _____ are in our National Museum.

3. Tutankhamen _____ Egypt as pharoah for a very short time before he died.

4. Your bike was stolen? You should _____ it to the police.

5. The _____ of Machu Picchu in Peru in 1911 caused a lot of excitement.

D Work with a partner. Discuss these questions.

CRITICAL THINKING: REFLECTING

1. What do you think King Tut probably looked like when he was alive?
2. King Tut's tomb was a major discovery. What are some other important discoveries that you know about?
3. What are some famous treasures from your country, and where can people go to see them?
4. What are some things you own that are precious to you? Explain.
5. What factors help you determine where to live? For example, is it more important to live in a place with good weather, or to live close to family members?
6. What are some things and places that you would like to investigate in order to learn more about them? Explain.

Listening A Conversation about an Assignment

BEFORE LISTENING

A Work with a partner. Read the notes that a college student wrote while watching a documentary film. Then talk about the documentary film.

> *The documentary was about the discovery of a historical site in Hanoi.*

Documentary Title: Uncovering the Past in Hanoi

- 2002, government plan - a new building in Hanoi, Vietnam
- They started construction, then found: ancient palaces & meeting halls & 1,000's of artifacts
- Name: Thang Long Imperial Citadel / (citadel = a safe place for royals)
- Gov't chose new site for its building; Thang Long Imperial Citadel now a UNESCO World Heritage site (popular for tourists)

WHILE LISTENING

LISTENING FOR
MAIN IDEAS

B 🎧 **Track 14** **Listen to the conversation. Choose the correct answers.**

1. The class assignment is to give an oral summary of a _____.

   a. movie or documentary film

   b. class lecture on the Thang Long Imperial Citadel

   c. historical site in Southeast Asia

2. Professor Norton told Silvio that _____.

   a. he should have taken a lot more notes

   b. his notes were not very helpful

   c. he had already begun to summarize the information

3. Professor Norton suggests that Silvio _____.

   a. write out his notes as complete sentences

   b. ask himself questions about the documentary he watched

   c. talk to some of the archaeologists on campus

4. Professor Norton says including a few examples can _____.

   a. make a summary very confusing

   b. help support the main ideas

   c. take too much time in a presentation

C 🔔 **Track 14** Look at the notes below for three key ideas from the conversation. Then listen again and take notes on the examples you hear for each key idea. Use indentation and *e.g,.* or *ex:* to indicate each example.

NOTE TAKING

1. Ruins found at hist. site in Hanoi, Vietnam

3. Archaeologists found many artifacts at site

2. Wh- question technique for summarizing

AFTER LISTENING

D Work with a partner. Compare and discuss your notes from exercise C. How do the examples that you recorded in your notes help you to understand the key ideas of the conversation?

The Imperial Citadel of Hanoi, Vietnam

B | Speaking

> **SPEAKING SKILL** Summarizing
>
> Summarizing means to briefly give the key points about something such as a movie, a book, an article, or a talk using your own words. When you give a summary, you should include only the most important information in order to answer the questions *Who, What, When, Where, How,* and *Why?* You should not include your own opinion in a summary—just the key facts about the topic.

NOTE TAKING

A 🎧 **Track 15** Listen to Silvio's oral summary of the documentary film he watched. As you listen, take brief notes in your notebook to answer each question.

1. Where was the site discovered?

2. When was it discovered?

3. How was it discovered?

4. Who was involved?

5. What did the Vietnamese government do, and why?

6. What happened in 2010?

CRITICAL THINKING:
EVALUATING

B Work with a partner. Compare your notes from exercise A. Then discuss Silvio's presentation. Do you think he did well on the oral-summary assignment? Explain.

CRITICAL THINKING:
APPLYING

C You are going to summarize the information about the San Bartolo discovery from Lesson A in this unit. Follow these steps.

1. Look back at the information about the San Bartolo discovery on page 24.
2. Decide which information you should include in a summary about the discovery. Use *wh-* questions to help you.
3. Use the chart below to take notes about the discovery. Use your own words.

Who?	*What?*	*When?*
Where?	*How?*	*Why?*

D Work with a partner. Take turns summarizing the information about the San Bartolo discovery. You can use your notes from exercise C to help you.

SUMMARIZING

E Think about your partner's summary from exercise D. Choose Y for *Yes* or N for *No* for each question. Then share and discuss your answers with your partner.

CRITICAL THINKING: EVALUATING

1. Did your partner answer the questions *Who, What, When, Where, How,* and *Why*?   Y   N
2. Was any important information missing?   Y   N
3. Did your partner include any unnecessary information?   Y   N
4. Did your partner include his or her opinion?   Y   N

FINAL TASK Giving a Presentation about a Historical Site

> You are going to give a short presentation about a historical site that interests you. It could be a place in your country that you have visited, or another place in the world.

A Brainstorm some interesting ancient or historical places in your country or in other parts of the world. Make a list in your notebook. Then choose one place you are interested in as the topic for your presentation.

BRAINSTORMING

The Great Wall of China

B If you need more information about your topic, do some research and take brief notes. Include the most important facts about the site and a few interesting details.

PRESENTATION SKILL Using Index Cards

Index cards can be useful for organizing your notes for a presentation. Here are some ways to use index cards when preparing for and giving a presentation:

- First, number your index cards. This will help you keep them in order later.
- Write only a few important ideas on each index card.
- Write only key words and phrases, not complete sentences.
- Practice your presentation using the index cards. Decide if you need to reorder any of the ideas in your presentation.
- As you present, look down at the cards only briefly to help you remember your ideas. Don't read directly from your cards.

C Prepare index cards to use during your presentation. Refer to the information in the Presentation Skill box to help you.

D Practice giving your presentation in front of a mirror or for friends or family members. After you finish, ask them these questions: *Were my ideas clear? Did I speak too quickly or too slowly?*

E Give your presentation to the class. When you give your presentation, remember to:

- Look at your notes or slides only occasionally.
- Look up and make eye contact with your audience.
- Ask your audience if they have any questions.

REFLECTION

1. How do you think you might use summarizing in the future?

_____

_____

2. Which ancient civilization from the unit was the most interesting to you? Why?

_____

_____

3. Here are the vocabulary words from the unit. Check (✓) the ones you can use.

☐ alive	☐ dig	☐ reveal AWL
☐ analyze AWL	☐ discovery	☐ royal
☐ ancient	☐ image AWL	☐ ruins
☐ archaeologist	☐ investigate AWL	☐ rule
☐ bury	☐ precious	☐ tomb
☐ civilization	☐ remains	☐ treasure
☐ determine	☐ report	

ENTREPRENEURS AND INNOVATORS

3

Mitsunobu Okada holds a model of the satellite ADRASI, which collects space garbage. Okada founded Astroscale, a start-up company committed to cleaning up trash in space.

ACADEMIC SKILLS

LISTENING	Distinguishing Facts and Opinions
	Reviewing and Editing Your Notes
SPEAKING	Rephrasing
	Thought Groups
CRITICAL THINKING	Interpreting Data

THINK AND DISCUSS

1 Look at the photo and read the caption. What does Okada's company do?

2 Look at the title of this unit. What are entrepreneurs and innovators? What do they do?

Look at the photos and read the information. Then discuss these questions.

1. What are some words you would use to describe entrepreneurs?
2. Which of the inventions or ideas on these pages do you find most interesting? Why?
3. Which of the inventions or ideas do you think is most useful? Least useful? Explain.
4. Would you like to be an entrepreneur? Why or why not?

THE ENTREPRENEURIAL SPIRIT

Designer Arturo Vittori stands near a WarkaWater tower, a lightweight structure that collects water from the air. Each tower costs about 500 US dollars and produces 90 liters of clean water per day.

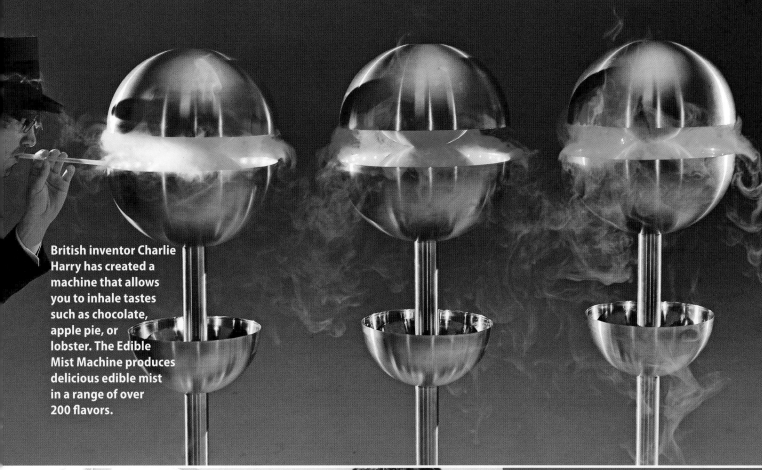

British inventor Charlie Harry has created a machine that allows you to inhale tastes such as chocolate, apple pie, or lobster. The Edible Mist Machine produces delicious edible mist in a range of over 200 flavors.

Archel Bernard teaches an employee how to use a sewing machine in her factory in Monrovia, Liberia. After she graduated from Georgia Tech, Bernard moved to Liberia where she opened her own boutique. She hopes to help Ebola survivors rebuild their lives.

An entrepreneur is someone who starts a business with a new idea, makes it grow, and takes the risk of failure. In general, entrepreneurs prefer to be their own bosses rather than working for someone else. The entrepreneurial spirit is a positive attitude toward risking time and money in order to find new and better ways of doing business.

A Vocabulary

MEANING FROM CONTEXT **A** 🎧 **Track 16** Read and listen to the information. Notice each word or phrase in **blue** and think about its meaning.

SIX TRAITS OF SUCCESSFUL ENTREPRENEURS

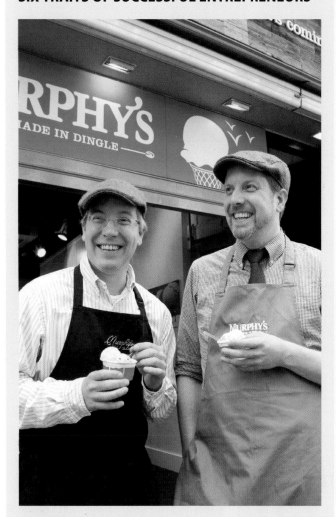

Brothers Kieran and Sean Murphy serve what is widely considered the best ice cream in Ireland.

What does it take to be a successful entrepreneur? Here are six common traits.

1. **Caring about More than Money:** Making money is usually not the main **motivation** for successful entrepreneurs. Instead, they are driven by a strong belief in their product or service and its potential to improve people's lives in some way.

2. **Not Giving Up:** Good entrepreneurs are **persistent**. They don't give up easily and are willing to try out new ideas and take risks. Doing this **leads to** some **failures** along the way, but the entrepreneurs who **eventually** succeed are the ones who do not quit when things go badly.

3. **Having a Vision:** True entrepreneurs see opportunities where most people do not. Then they need to convince **investors** to lend money for new kinds of products and services.

4. **Dealing with Change:** Being open-minded and flexible is another important trait for entrepreneurs. The product they imagined in the beginning is likely to **evolve** over time, so they need to be flexible.

5. **Tolerating Uncertainty:** Entrepreneurs must be able to live with **uncertainty**. Nobody can predict the future, but good entrepreneurs keep moving ahead with their ideas rather than worrying about the unknown.

6. **Having Self-Confidence:** The sixth **essential** trait of successful entrepreneurs is psychological—having **confidence** in oneself. The best entrepreneurs believe in themselves and their ideas.

B Choose T for *True* or F for *False* for each statement. Correct the false statements.

1. Your motivation is your reason for doing something.   T   F

2. A persistent person will try and try again.   T   F

3. If one thing leads to a second thing, it causes the second thing to happen.   T   F

4. Failures in business are when things go well and you get what you want.   T   F

5. Events that happen eventually happen very soon. T   F

6. Investors are people who lend you money that you must pay back later. T   F

7. When something evolves over time, it stays the same. T   F

8. If we have uncertainty about something, we are not sure about it. T   F

9. If something is essential, you don't really need it. T   F

10. People with a lot of confidence feel sure about themselves and their abilities. T   F

C Work with a partner. Take turns asking and answering these questions.

CRITICAL THINKING: REFLECTING

1. What are three things that are essential for your happiness? Why are they so important to you?

2. Talk about a time you chose to do something challenging. What was your motivation for doing it?

3. People's ideas and opinions often change during their lives. How have your ideas and opinions evolved over the years?

VOCABULARY SKILL Recognizing Adjectives and Adverbs

Recognizing different word forms such as adjectives and adverbs can help you expand your vocabulary and better understand information you hear and read.

Adjectives describe or modify nouns.

> A **persistent** <u>businessperson</u> will last longer than any **temporary** <u>problem</u>.

Common adjective suffixes include:

> -al (personal)   -ous (famous)   -ary (voluntary)   -ant/-ent (reluctant)
> -able (sociable)

Adverbs describe or modify verbs, adjectives, or other adverbs.

> We **eventually** <u>found</u> the office even though the door was not **well** <u>marked</u>.

Most adverbs have an -ly suffix, but irregular adverbs include very, almost, well, and too.

D Choose the correct words to complete the sentences. Then work with a partner and compare your answers.

1. I recently applied for a (permanent / permanently) position in the company's (regional / regionally) office.

2. The job interview went (good / well), even though I didn't feel (confident / confidently) at first.

3. The company is looking for a (persistent / persistently) salesperson who doesn't give up easily. The (ideal / ideally) candidate will have at least five years of sales experience.

4. The job requires a (capable / capably) person who can work (independent / independently). It's currently a part-time postion, but it may (eventual / eventually) become full time.

5. This is a (perfect / perfectly) job for a (high / highly) qualified person. The salary and benefits are very (good / well), too.

A Listening A Presentation about a Success Story

BEFORE LISTENING

PRIOR KNOWLEDGE **A** Discuss these questions with a partner.

1. What are some large, successful companies you know about? What do you think makes these companies so successful?
2. When you purchase a product, for example, a phone or a new pair of shoes, how do you decide which item to buy?

WHILE LISTENING

LISTENING FOR
MAIN IDEAS **B** 🎧 **Track 17** ▶ **3.1** Listen to the presentation. Which of these points does the speaker make? Choose Y for *Yes* or N for *No* for each statement.

1. Howard Schultz wanted to bring European coffee culture to the United States.   Y   N

2. It was difficult for Schultz to find investors for his company.   Y   N

3. Starbucks' profits are mostly due to the high quality of its coffee drinks.   Y   N

4. Starbucks employees earn more than workers in other service jobs.   Y   N

5. The company had problems after Schultz quit his job in 2000.   Y   N

6. Schultz plans to remain the CEO of the company until he retires.   Y   N

LISTENING SKILL Distinguishing Facts and Opinions

When listening to a talk or lecture, it is important to be able to distinguish facts from opinions.

Facts are statements that can be proved or verified. We can do this by checking several reliable sources of information.

Fact: *The people who work at Starbucks are called "partners" rather than "employees."*

Opinions show a speaker's viewpoint or bias. It is possible to disagree with someone's opinion.

Opinion: *I guess Starbucks wants to show its employees how important they are to the company.*

Here are some common expressions used for giving opinions:

For me, . . .	*If you ask me, . . .*	*Personally, . . .*	*I believe . . .*
I think . . .	*In my opinion, . . .*	*I guess . . .*	

C 🎧 **Track 17** Listen again and complete the statements from the talk. Fill in each blank with the two words that you hear.

1. And although _____ isn't actually "little" anymore, it did start out that way.

2. Now, of course, _____ like the world was just waiting for a good caffè latte to come along.

3. If you _____, focusing only on making money is a great way to make a business fail.

4. Not only are Starbucks wages a little higher than in other service jobs, partners who work enough hours can _____ in the company.

5. I mean— _____ is that?

6. Schultz has given up his position as CEO on more than one occasion over the years. The first time was _____.

D Work with a partner. Compare your answers from exercise C and decide whether each statement is a fact or an opinion. How do you know?

AFTER LISTENING

E Work in a group. Discuss the meaning of each idea from a business point of view. Do you agree or disagree with each statement? Explain.

1. The customer is always right.
2. Constant improvement is the way to success in business.
3. People who don't wait for someone to tell them what to do make more money.
4. In business, we spend too much time on what is urgent and not enough time on what is important.

A Speaking

GRAMMAR FOR SPEAKING The Present Perfect and Signal Words

We use the present perfect to talk about:

1. actions or situations that began in the past and continue until now.

   Lydia's parents **have worked** *there for 20 years.* (They still work there now.)

2. actions or situations that have happened one or more times in the past and relate to the present. The exact time that the action or situation happened is not stated or important.

   Schultz **has quit** *his position as CEO twice in the past 20 years.*

   We **have** *never* **gone** *to a business conference before, so we want to go to one.*

We often use signal words and phrases with the present perfect to give extra information about when something happened or about the speaker's attitude. Here are some examples of signal words and phrases that are commonly used with the present perfect:

for	*since*	*already*	*so far*	*(not) yet*
up to now	*ever*	*never*	*always*	

   We're a new company, but we **have already grown** *a lot.* (We've grown faster than I expected.)

   We **have earned** *profits totaling $71,000* **so far** *this year.* (We might still earn more.)

   Has *it really* **been** *five years* **since** *the company introduced a new product?* (Was the last time really five years ago?)

   Have *you* **ever eaten** *at that restaurant?* (Have you eaten there at any time in the past?)

A Complete the sentences using the present perfect form of the verbs and the signal words in parentheses.

1. Rosa _____ (be) the bank manager since 2013.

2. I _____ (call) customer service three times, and they still _____ (not, answer) the telephone.

3. _____ you _____ (ever, stay) at that hotel before? Is it a nice place?

4. Nabil _____ (always, want) to open his own furniture store.

5. We _____ (own) the restaurant for 17 years.

6. I _____ (buy) coffee at that shop several times, and so far the service _____ (be) fast and friendly. It _____ (never, be) slow.

7. Sandra _____ (work) at the same company for 25 years.

8. I _____ (not, send) the report yet, but I'll do it today.

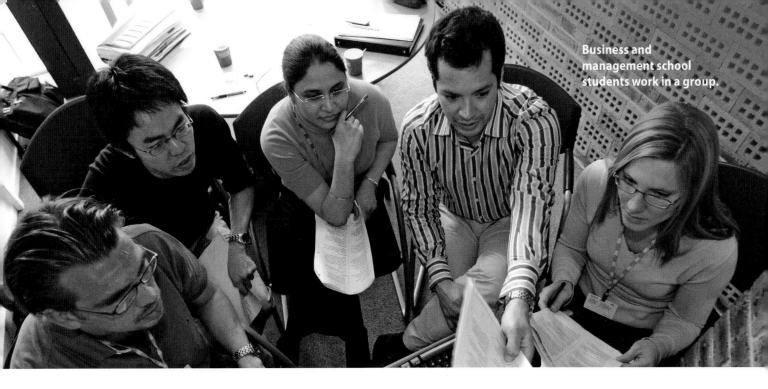

Business and management school students work in a group.

B Work with a partner. Take turns asking and answering questions about the topics below. Use *ever* and the present perfect in your questions. Give details about your answers to keep the conversation going.

A: *Have you ever taken a class in business or economics?*
B: *No, I haven't, but I'd like to.*

1. take a class in business or economics
2. buy a coffee drink at Starbucks
3. visit your country's capital city
4. get paid for your work
5. be interviewed for a job
6. think about starting your own company

PRONUNCIATION Thought Groups

🎧 **Track 18** In English, speakers organize their ideas into chunks or *thought groups*. Thought groups can consist of a single word (*Exactly!*), a phrase (*for 20 years*), a clause (*The company experienced . . .*), or a short sentence (*It's a beautiful city.*). Each thought group usually has one focus word. There is a slight pause between thoughts groups. Using thought groups will make your speech sound more fluent and will help your listeners understand you.

> *In the early days, / Schultz was like / every entrepreneur.*
> *The company experienced / some major problems / as a result.*

C 🎧 **Track 19** Listen to each statement, and put a slash (/) at the end of each thought group you hear. Then practice saying the sentences with a partner. Use thought groups.

1. My best friend started her own company about five years ago right after college.
2. Her son wants to study business and then work at a bank.
3. Running a successful business is not easy because you work a lot and have to take risks.
4. I got a job at the new café on Main Street.
5. If you work hard and treat people well you'll be successful.
6. After work I usually take a walk so I can relax and get some exercise.

ENTREPRENEURS AND INNOVATORS **49**

Rephrasing means repeating the same information or idea using different words. We use rephrasing for clarification and emphasis.

> A: *I haven't seen Masayo in ages.*
> B: *I'm sorry… I didn't understand.*
> A: *It's been a long time since I saw your brother.*

We sometimes use these expressions when rephrasing.

> *In other words, …*   *To clarify, …*   *What I mean is …*   *That is, …*

REPHRASING

D Work with a partner. Take turns saying each sentence and then rephrasing it in a new way.

> **>** *I need to get something to eat. In other words, I'm hungry.*

1. I need to get something to eat.
2. What's your motivation for learning English?
3. Our English teacher knows a lot about grammar.
4. I'm interested in starting my own business.
5. Do you have a lot of self-confidence?
6. I have never shopped online.

E Work with a partner. Partner A will read Part A of the article about the city of Detroit. Partner B will read Part B.

PART A

The city of Detroit in the United States used to be called "the motor city." It was the home of the American automobile industry, and Ford, Chrysler, and General Motors all had enormous factories there. Jobs were not hard to find, and they came with high wages and good benefits such as health insurance and time off with pay.

PART B

However, since the 1970s, Detroit has lost thousands of jobs. Many people have left the city, and neighborhoods are full of empty houses. Poverty and crime are serious problems in Detroit as well. Recently, though, entrepreneurs are finding new opportunities here. They are buying inexpensive homes and businesses and turning them into success stories through their persistence and hard work.

George Higgins plays piano and sings in downtown Detroit.

F With your partner, take turns retelling your part of the article about Detriot. Practice rephrasing.

REPHRASING

G Discuss these questions with your partner.

PERSONALIZING

1. What interests you about the information in the article? What surprises you?
2. What city or cities in your country are doing well economically? What kind of work do people do there?

LESSON TASK Interpreting Quotations

A Work in a group. Read the quotations below from famous entrepreneurs and innovators, and discuss these questions.

CRITICAL THINKING: INTERPRETING QUOTATIONS

1. What do you think each quotation means? How might you rephrase it in your own words?
2. Discuss whether you agree or disagree with each quotation. Use examples from your own life to explain and support your ideas.
3. What do you know about each of these entrepreneurs and innovators? Which person do you find most interesting? Explain.

a. Henry Ford (automobile manufacturer): *"The short successes that can be gained in a brief time and without difficulty are not worth much."*

b. Nikola Tesla (engineer and inventor): *"Be alone, that is the secret of invention; be alone, that is when ideas are born."*

c. Marissa Meyer (CEO of Yahoo): *"When you need to innovate, you need collaboration[1]."*

d. Marie Curie (physicist and chemist): *"I was taught that the way of progress is neither swift[2] nor easy."*

e. Albert Einstein (theoretical physicist): *"Play is the highest form of research."*

f. Steve Jobs (co-founder of Apple): *"Being the richest man in the cemetery[3] doesn't matter to me. Going to bed at night saying we've done something wonderful—that's what matters to me."*

[1]**collaboration** (n): working together to accomplish a goal
[2]**swift** (adj): fast
[3]**cemetery** (n): a place where dead people are buried

B Discuss some other famous entrepreneurs and innovators that you know about.

CRITICAL THINKING: REFLECTING

Video

National Geographic Explorer Sanga Moses's goal is to provide inexpensive cooking fuel for Africans while improving socioeconomic outcomes and reversing deforestation.

Eco-Fuel Africa

Uganda

BEFORE VIEWING

A Read the information about Sanga Moses. Then with a partner, discuss how you think a "social entrepreneur" differs from other entepreneurs.

> **MEET SANGA MOSES.** He's a National Geographic Explorer and a social entrepreneur who quit a job at a bank in Kampala—Uganda's capital city—in order to work on solving a real problem in his country. He saw that girls, especially, had to find and carry wood for fuel intead of spending their time at school. Today, thousands of families in Uganda use Moses's clean-burning cooking fuel every day. And because the fuel is made from farm waste[1], for example, from corn crops, around 3,000 farmers and retailers[2] earn extra income each month by working with Moses's company, Eco-Fuel Africa.

[1]**farm waste** (n): parts of crop plants not used for food
[2]**retailers** (n): people who sell products to the public

PERSONALIZING   **B** Work with a partner. Discuss these questions.

1. When you were a child, did you have household chores to do? For example, did you do some of the shopping, cleaning, or cooking for your family?
2. In your country, what kind of fuel do most people use for cooking? Do you think the fuel is convenient? Environmentally friendly? Is it expensive or inexpensive?

WHILE VIEWING

C ▶ 3.2 Read the statements. Then watch the video and choose the correct word to complete each statement.

UNDERSTANDING MAIN IDEAS

1. Moses got the idea for his company when he saw his (sister / brother) carrying wood.
2. When he quit his job at the bank, people were (upset / shocked).
3. He sold his (furniture / car).
4. Moses is now the (president / CEO) of Eco-Fuel Africa.
5. His advice is to (listen to / follow) your heart and believe in your dreams.

D ▶ 3.2 Watch the video again and fill in each blank with the number that you hear.

UNDERSTANDING DETAILS

1. After _____ months, Moses had spent all of his savings.

2. Eco-Fuel is _____ percent cheaper than other fuels.

3. Today, about _____ families use Moses's product.

4. Moses's goal in the next _____ years is to reach _____ million families.

AFTER VIEWING

CRITICAL THINKING   Interpreting Data

Interpreting data can increase your knowledge and understanding of a topic. To interpret data, look at the title and categories of the information included. Then look at the numbers and ask yourself questions such as: *What information does this data provide? How is this data important or relevant to the topic or situation?*

E Work in a group. Look at the data about Uganda and discuss the questions below.

CRITICAL THINKING: INTERPRETING DATA

Data about Uganda

Population: around 35 million

Percent of Population Under 30 Years Old: 78%

Literacy Rate: 78% (male 85%, female 72%)

Access to Electricity: 20% of households

Cooking Fuel: 94% use firewood or charcoal

Percent of Households Involved in Agriculture: 80%

---

1. Based on your knowledge or an Internet search, how does this data compare with the numbers for your country? For example, does your country have a smaller or larger population than Uganda?
2. What do you notice about the literacy rate in Uganda? How does this information support Sanga Moses's concern about his sister not spending time at school?
3. How does the data help you understand information from the video?

Vocabulary

A 🎧 **Track 20** Read and listen to the information. Notice each word in blue and think about its meaning.

CHANDA SHROFF

When Chanda Shroff visited a part of India known as Kutch, she saw the **potential** for village women there to earn an **income** by selling their beautiful embroidery[1] work. Shroff thought there was a strong **probability** that other people would **appreciate** the beautiful embroidery as much as she did, so she commissioned[2] 30 embroidered *saris*[3] before she left Kutch. **Evidently**, she was right. The saris caused **considerable** excitement at an art exhibit in Mumbai. Shroff sold all 30 of them within a few hours.

▲ **Social entrepreneur Chanda Shroff, 1933–2016**

Kutch, India

Shroff eventually **founded** an innovative organization called Shrujan. Its **mission** is to market this traditional craft and help the Kutch people become more self-sufficient and to keep the craft alive and evolving. Since the Shrujan organization was founded, it has helped over 22,000 women earn sustainable, home-based income for their work and **achieve** more financial security. Shrujan has received a lot of **recognition** for its work, and Shroff herself received a Rolex Award for Enterprise in 2006. Shroff died in 2016, but the Kutch people still love and respect this woman who made a significant difference in so many people's lives.

[1] **embroidery** (n): decorative work done with a needle and colorful thread
[2] **commissioned** (v): formally asked for something to be done
[3] **saris** (n): traditional clothing worn by women in southern Asia

B Write each word in blue from exercise A next to its definition.

1. _____ (n) the chance that something will happen

2. _____ (v) to reach something positive such as success or happiness

3. _____ (n) credit or praise for doing something well

4. _____ (n) the possibility of being or doing something

5. _____ (n) money earned from working, investments, etc.

6. _____ (adv) as it appears, seemingly

7. _____ (v) to value or be thankful for something

8. _____ (v) started an organization

9. _____ (adj) much, a lot

10. _____ (n) the goals and purpose of a person, organization, or business

Young women sewing in
Kutch, Gujarat, India

C Read each statement and choose T for *True* or F for *False*. Correct the false statements.

1. If there is a strong probability of rain tomorrow, you should carry an umbrella.　　　　T　　F

2. If a company earns considerable profits, they are not making much money.　　　　T　　F

3. Someone who founded a company closed it down.　　　　T　　F

4. Investors will probably not lend you money if your company has the potential to succeed.　　　　T　　F

5. People who have achieved a lot in their lives usually feel good about themselves.　　　　T　　F

D Work with a partner. Discuss these questions.

CRITICAL THINKING:
ANALYZING

1. In your own words, describe what Chanda Shroff achieved.
2. Do you think Chanda Shroff's mission is similar to Sanga Moses's? To Howard Schultz's? Explain.
3. One way that Shroff was innovative was in creating a completely new way for people to earn money. How do you think the new income has affected people's lives?

Listening A Conversation about Jack Andraka

BEFORE LISTENING

A Read the information. Then discuss the questions below with a partner.

> **JACK ANDRAKA** is a National Geographic Explorer who developed a test that can detect[1] certain types of cancer. He has won several awards for the test and has been a guest at the White House. He has been on TV shows and has been the subject of documentary films.
>
> Andraka invented the cancer test when he was only 15 years old. His motivation was the death of a close family friend from pancreatic cancer. Thanks to Andraka's work, doctors will soon be able to test for that type of cancer more cheaply and accurately, and they'll be able to detect the cancer much sooner.

[1]**detect** (v): to find or notice something

1. Have you heard about Jack Andraka before? If so, what do you know about him?
2. Why do you think he is getting so much recognition for his work?
3. Andraka had a strong motivation for trying to do something about cancer. What other innovative people can you think of who wanted to solve a problem?

National Geographic Explorer Jack Andraka works in his lab. Andraka created a new test for detecting pancreatic, lung, and ovarian cancer.

WHILE LISTENING

B 🎧 **Track 21** Listen to the conversation and complete the notes about Jack Andraka.

LISTENING FOR
MAIN IDEAS

Jack Andraka's mission: find _____

If Dr.s detect cancer early → higher probability treated and _____

Andraka's test: 1. cheap (costs _____)   2. fast (takes _____)

        3. better than existing test; existing test = _____ + _____

Test not available yet (still needs _____)

C 🎧 **Track 21** Listen to the conversation again. Add any important details about Jack Andraka to the main ideas you wrote in exercise B.

LISTENING FOR
DETAILS

AFTER LISTENING

> **NOTE-TAKING SKILL** Reviewing and Editing Your Notes
>
> As soon as possible after you have taken notes, read through them and think about the information you heard in the talk or discussion. Doing this will confirm your understanding and help you remember the information later and for longer. As you review your notes, you can also do some editing to ensure the notes will be useful to you later. Here are some ways to do this:
>
> - Add any information that is missing.
> - Rewrite or replace any notes that are difficult to read.
> - Use highlighters to mark key ideas and important details.

D Review and edit the notes you took in exercises B and C. Follow the suggestions from the Note-Taking Skill box.

E Work with a partner. Compare your edited notes from exercise D. Did you miss any important information? If so, add it to your notes.

F With your partner, discuss the different aspects of Jack Andraka's achievement. Rank them in order (1–4) of how impressive or important they seem to you (1 = the highest; 4 = the lowest).

CRITICAL THINKING:
RANKING

_____ Andraka's age   _____ being able to detect cancers earlier

_____ the low cost of the test   _____ the short time the test takes

G Form a group with another pair of students. Compare and discuss how you ranked the factors in exercise F.

B Speaking

We use the infinitive of purpose to give a reason or purpose for doing something. The infinitive of purpose can come at the beginning or end of a sentence.

*Elias borrowed a lot of money **in order to start** his new business.*
*Elias borrowed a lot of money **to start** his new business.*

***In order to get** a good grade, Freya studied for nine hours before the test.*
***To get** a good grade, Freya studied for nine hours before the test.*

A With your partner, think of one or more ways to complete each statement using infinitives to show purpose.

> *Howard Schultz chooses to pay employees a little more to make their lives better.*

1. Howard Schultz chooses to pay employees a little more . . .
2. Starbucks partners write the customer's name on the coffee cup . . .
3. Chanda Shroff commissioned 30 saris from Kutch women . . .
4. Shroff founded the Shrujan organization . . .
5. Jack Andraka invented a new cancer test . . .
6. The test uses a special kind of paper . . .
7. Many people become doctors…
8. People go to business school…
9. We are meeting with potential investors…
10. The company hired ten new sales people…

B Work with a partner. Take turns asking and answering the questions. Use infinitives to show purpose in your answers.

> *People take test preparation courses to improve their test scores.*

1. Why do people take test preparation courses?
2. Why do people spend time with their friends?
3. Why do businesses have to advertise?
4. Why do people drink coffee or tea in the morning?
5. Why do people go to the library?
6. Why do you take notes in class?
7. Why are you learning English?
8. Why do you use the Internet?
9. Think of one of the apps on your phone. Why do you use it?
10. Think of a popular tourist spot in your country. Why do people visit it?

FINAL TASK Presenting a New Product

You are going to participate in a role-play about an innovative product. First, with a partner, you are going to think of an innovative product or service. Then you will present your idea to another pair of students who will play the role of potential investors. You will ask the investors for money in order to start your new business. The investors will consider your idea carefully and decide whether or not to lend you the money you need.

A Work with a partner. Brainstorm a list of ideas for new products or services. Discuss these questions to help you get started. Write your ideas in your notebook.

BRAINSTORMING

1. What kinds of problems or difficulties do you experience in your everyday life at home or at school? What kind of product or service might solve some of those problems?
2. What are some problems that employees at schools, hospitals, offices, and other workplaces experience? What product or service could improve those people's lives?
3. What are some problems in cities or in the natural environment? What product or service could help to solve those problems?

> **EVERYDAY LANGUAGE**   Complimenting Someone's Work
>
> *Good job!*   *I like that idea!*   *Great idea!*
> *That was an interesting presentation!*

▽ **Edwin Van Ruymbeke, inventor and developer of the Bionic Bird, a flying toy that can be operated by smartphone, holds one of his bird-shaped drones.**

B With your partner, look at your list of ideas from exercise A and decide which product or service you want to present. Then complete your business proposal.

Business Proposal

Name of product or service: _____

Purpose of the product or service: _____

How much will it cost? _____

Who will want to buy it, and why? _____

How will you market it? _____

Will the product or service need to be tested? Manufactured? How much money do you need from investors to get started with your business?

_____

PRESENTATION SKILL Thinking about Your Audience

When you give a presentation, thinking about your audience can help you decide which information to include and how best to present that information. Here are some questions you can ask yourself when you are preparing for a presentation.

- *Who is my audience? What do I know about them?*
- *What do they already know about my topic?*
- *What do they want to learn or gain from my presentation?*

C Practice your presentation. Your audience will be potential investors for your new product or service. Think about your audience as you practice your presentation.

D Form a group with another pair of students. Follow these instructions.

1. Pair A: Present your proposal for an innovative product or service to the investors. Ask them for the money you need to start your new business.
2. Pair B: Listen to the entrepreneurs' presentation. Decide if you will lend them the money for their new product or service. Explain your decision.
3. Switch roles and repeat.

REFLECTION

1. What techniques did you learn to help you with note taking?

_____

_____

2. Which entrepreneur or innovator in the unit was the most interesting to you? Why?

_____

_____

3. Here are the vocabulary words and phrases from the unit. Check (✓) the ones you can use.

☐ achieve AWL	☐ evolve AWL	☐ motivation AWL
☐ appreciate AWL	☐ failure	☐ persistent AWL
☐ confidence	☐ found AWL	☐ potential AWL
☐ considerable AWL	☐ income AWL	☐ probability
☐ essential	☐ investor AWL	☐ recognition
☐ eventually AWL	☐ lead to	☐ uncertainty
☐ evidently AWL	☐ mission	

Independent Student Handbook

Table of Contents

Listening Skills	page 61
Note-Taking Skills	page 63
Organizing Information	page 64
Speaking: Phrases for Classroom Communication	page 66
Speaking: Phrases for Presenting	page 68
Presentation Strategies	page 69
Presentation Outline	page 71
Pronunciation Guide	page 72
Vocabulary Building Strategies	page 73

LISTENING SKILLS

Predicting

Speakers giving formal talks usually begin by introducing themselves and their topic. Listen carefully to the introduction of the topic so that you can predict what the talk will be about.

Strategies:

- Use visual information including titles on the board or on presentation slides.
- Think about what you already know about the topic.
- Ask yourself questions that you think the speaker might answer.
- Listen for specific phrases that indicate an introduction (e.g., *My topic is…*).

Listening for Main Ideas

It's important to be able to tell the difference between a speaker's main ideas and supporting details. It is more common for teachers to test students' understanding of main ideas than of specific details.

Strategies:

- Listen carefully to the introduction. Speakers often state the main idea in the introduction.
- Listen for rhetorical questions, or questions that the speaker asks, and then answers. Often the answer is the statement of the main idea.
- Notice words and phrases that the speaker repeats. Repetition often signals main ideas.

Listening for Details (Examples)

A speaker often provides examples that support a main idea. A good example can help you understand and remember the main idea better.

Strategies:

- Listen for specific phrases that introduce examples.
- Listen for general statements. Examples often follow general statements.

Listening for Details (Reasons)

Speakers often give reasons or list causes and/or effects to support their ideas.

Strategies:

- Notice nouns that might signal causes/reasons (e.g., *factors, influences, causes, reasons*) or effects/results (e.g., *effects, results, outcomes, consequences*).
- Notice verbs that might signal causes/reasons (e.g., *contribute to, affect, influence, determine, produce, result in*) or effects/results (often these are passive, e.g., *is affected by*).

Understanding the Structure of a Presentation

An organized speaker uses expressions to alert the audience to important information that will follow. Recognizing signal words and phrases will help you understand how a presentation is organized and the relationship between ideas.

Introduction

A good introduction identifies the topic and gives an idea of how the lecture or presentation will be organized. Here are some expressions to introduce a topic:

I'll be talking about …   *My topic is …*

There are basically two groups … *There are three reasons …*

Body

In the body of a lecture, speakers usually expand upon the topic. They often use phrases that signal the order of events or subtopics and their relationship to each other. Here are some expressions to help listeners follow the body of a lecture:

The first/next/final (point/reason) is … *First/Next/Finally, let's look at …*

Another reason is …   *However, …*

Conclusion

In the conclusion of a lecture, speakers often summarize what they have said. They may also make predictions or suggestions. Sometimes they ask a question in the conclusion to get the audience to think more about the topic. Here are some expressions to give a conclusion:

In conclusion, …   *In summary, …*

As you can see. . .   *To review, + (restatement of main points)*

Understanding Meaning from Context

When you are not familiar with a word that a speaker says, you can sometimes guess the meaning of the word or fill in the gaps using the context or situation itself.

Strategies:

- Don't panic. You don't always understand every word of what a speaker says in your first language, either.
- Use context clues to fill in the blanks. What did you understand just before or just after the missing part? What did the speaker probably say?
- Listen for words and phrases that signal a definition or explanation (e.g., *What that means is…*).

Recognizing a Speaker's Bias

Speakers often have an opinion about the topic they are discussing. It's important for you to know if they are objective or subjective about the topic. Objective speakers do not express an opinion. Subjective speakers have a bias or a strong feeling about the topic.

Strategies:

- Notice words like adjectives, adverbs, and modals that the speaker uses (e.g., *ideal, horribly, should, shouldn't*). These suggest that the speaker has a bias.
- Listen to the speaker's voice. Does he or she sound excited, angry, or bored?
- Notice if the speaker gives more weight or attention to one point of view over another.
- Listen for words that signal opinions (e.g., *I think…*).

NOTE-TAKING SKILLS

Taking notes is a personalized skill. It is important to develop a note-taking system that works for you. However, there are some common strategies to improve your note taking.

Before You Listen

Focus

Try to clear your mind before the speaker begins so you can pay attention. If possible, review previous notes or think about what you already know about the topic.

Predict

If you know the topic of the talk, think about what you might hear.

Listen

Take Notes by Hand

Research suggests that taking notes by hand rather than on a computer is more effective. Taking notes by hand requires you to summarize, rephrase, and synthesize information. This helps you *encode* the information, or put it into a form that you can understand and remember.

Listen for Signal Words and Phrases

Speakers often use signal words and phrases (e.g., *Today we're going to talk about…*) to organize their ideas and show relationships between them. Listening for signal words and phrases can help you decide what information to write in your notes.

Condense (Shorten) Information

- As you listen, focus on the most important ideas. The speaker will usually repeat, define, explain, and/or give examples of these ideas. Take notes on these ideas.

    Speaker: *The Itaipu Dam provides about 20% of the electricity used in Brazil, and about 75% of the electricity used in Paraguay. That electricity goes to millions of homes and businesses, so it's good for the economy of both countries.*

    Notes: Itaipu Dam → electricity: Brazil 20%, Paraguay 75%

- Don't write full sentences. Write only key words (nouns, verbs, adjectives, and adverbs), phrases, or short sentences.

    Full sentence: *Teachers are normally at the top of the list of happiest jobs.*

    Notes: teachers happiest

- Leave out information that is obvious.

  Full sentence: *Photographer Annie Griffiths is famous for her beautiful photographs. She travels all over the world to take photos.*

  Notes: *A. Griffiths travels world*
- Write numbers and statistics. (*9 bil; 35%*)
- Use abbreviations (e.g., *ft., min., yr*) and symbols (=, ≠, >, <, %, →)
- Use indenting. Write main ideas on the left side of the paper. Indent details.
    Benefits of eating ugly foods
      Save $
        10-20% on ugly fruits & vegs. at market
- Write details under key terms to help you remember them.
- Write the definitions of important new words.

After You Listen

- Review your notes soon after the lecture or presentation. Add any details you missed.
- Clarify anything you don't understand in your notes with a classmate or teacher.
- Add or highlight main ideas. Cross out details that aren't important or necessary.
- Rewrite anything that is hard to read or understand. Rewrite your notes in an outline or other graphic organizer to organize the information more clearly.
- Use arrows, boxes, diagrams, or other visual cues to show relationships between ideas.

ORGANIZING INFORMATION

You can use a graphic organizer to take notes while you are listening, or to organize your notes after you listen. Here are some examples of graphic organizers:

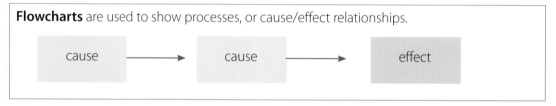

Flowcharts are used to show processes, or cause/effect relationships.

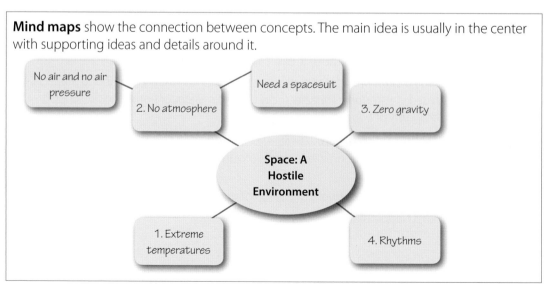

Mind maps show the connection between concepts. The main idea is usually in the center with supporting ideas and details around it.

Outlines show the relationship between main ideas and details.

To use an outline for taking notes, write the main ideas at the left margin of your paper. Below the main ideas, indent and write the supporting ideas and details. You may do this as you listen, or go back and rewrite your notes as an outline later.

I. **Introduction:** How to feed the world

II. **Steps**

    Step One: Stop deforestation

        a. stop burning rainforests

        b. grow crops on land size of South America

T-charts compare two topics.

Climate Change in Greenland	
Benefits	**Drawbacks**
shorter winters	rising sea levels

Timelines show a sequence of events.

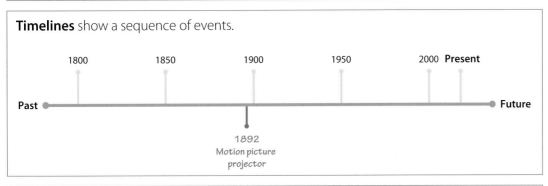

Venn diagrams compare and contrast two or more topics. The overlapping areas show similarities.

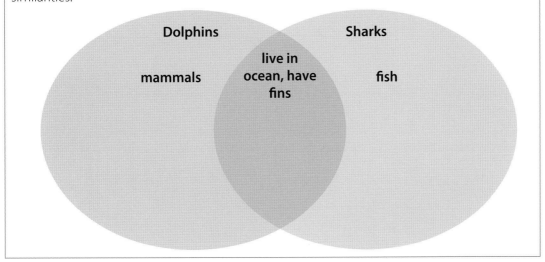

SPEAKING: PHRASES FOR CLASSROOM COMMUNICATION

Phrases for Expressing Yourself	
Expressing Opinions *I think…* *I believe…* *I'm sure…* *In my opinion/view…* *If you ask me,…* *Personally,…* *To me,…*	**Expressing Likes and Dislikes** *I like…* *I prefer…* *I love…* *I can't stand…* *I hate…* *I really don't like…* *I don't care for…*
Giving Facts *There is evidence/proof…* *Experts claim/argue…* *Studies show…* *Researchers found…* *The record shows…*	**Giving Tips or Suggestions** *Imperatives (e.g., Try to get more sleep.)* *You/We should/shouldn't…* *You/We ought to…* *It's (not) a good idea to…* *I suggest (that)…* *Let's…* *How about… + (noun/gerund)* *What about… + (noun/gerund)* *Why don't we/you…* *You/We could…*
Agreeing *I agree.* *True.* *Good point.* *Exactly.* *Absolutely.* *I was just about to say that.* *Definitely.* *Right!*	**Disagreeing** *I disagree.* *I'm not so sure about that.* *I don't know.* *That's a good point, but I don't agree.* *I see what you mean, but I think that…*

Phrases for Interacting with Others

Clarifying/Checking Your Understanding

So are you saying that…?
So what you mean is…?
What do you mean?
How's that?
How so?
I'm not sure I understand/follow.
Do you mean…?
I'm not sure what you mean.

Asking for Clarification/Confirming Understanding

Sorry, I didn't catch that. Could you repeat it?
I'm not sure I understand the question.
I'm not sure I understand what you mean.
Sorry, I'm not following you.
Are you saying that…?
If I understand correctly, you're saying that…
Oh, now I get it. You're talking about…, right?

Checking Others' Understanding

Does that make sense?
Do you understand?
Do you see what I mean?
Is that clear?
Are you following/with me?
Do you have any questions?

Asking for Opinions

What do you think?
We haven't heard from you in a while.
Do you have anything to add?
What are your thoughts?
How do you feel?
What's your opinion?

Taking Turns

Can/May I say something?
Could I add something?
Can I just say…?
May I continue?
Can I finish what I was saying?
Did you finish your thought?
Let me finish.
Let's get back to…

Interrupting Politely

Excuse me.
Pardon me.
Forgive me for interrupting…
I hate to interrupt but…
Can I stop you for a second?

Asking for Repetition

Could you say that again?
I'm sorry?
I didn't catch what you said.
I'm sorry. I missed that. What did you say?
Could you repeat that please?

Showing Interest

I see.	*Good for you.*
Really?	*Seriously?*
Um-hmm.	*No kidding!*
Wow.	*And? (Then what?)*
That's funny / amazing / incredible / awful!	

SPEAKING: PHRASES FOR PRESENTING

Introduction

Introducing a Topic

I'm going to talk about…
My topic is…
I'm going to present…
I plan to discuss…
Let's start with…

Today we're going to talk about…
So we're going to show you…
Now/Right/So/Well, (pause), *let's look at…*
There are three groups/reasons/effects/factors…
There are four steps in this process.

Body

Listing or Sequencing

First/First of all/The first (noun)/To start/To begin,…
Second/Secondly/The second/Next/Another/Also/Then/In addition,…
Last/The last/Finally,…
There are many/several/three types/kinds of/ways,…

Signaling Problems/Solutions

One problem/issue/challenge is…
One solution/answer/response is…

Giving Reasons or Causes

Because + (clause): Because the climate is changing…
Because of + (noun phrase): Because of climate change…
Due to + (noun phrase)…
Since + (clause)
The reason that I like hip-hop is…
One reason that people listen to music is…
One factor is + (noun phrase)
The main reason that…

Giving Results or Effects

so + (clause): so I went to the symphony
Therefore, + (sentence): Therefore, I went to the symphony.
As a result, + (sentence).
Consequently, + (sentence).
…causes + (noun phrase)
…leads to + (noun phrase)
…had an impact/effect on + (noun phrase)
If…then…

Giving Examples

The first example is…
Here's an example of what I mean…
For instance,…
For example,…
Let me give you an example…
…such as…
…like…

Repeating and Rephrasing

What you need to know is…
I'll say this again…
So again, let me repeat…
The most important point is…

Signaling Additional Examples or Ideas	Signaling to Stop Taking Notes
Not only…but,	*You don't need this for the test.*
Besides…	*This information is in your books/on your handout/on the website.*
Not only do…, but also	*You don't have to write all this down.*
Identifying a Side Track	**Returning to a Previous Topic**
This is off-topic,…	*Getting back to our previous discussion,…*
On a different subject,…	*To return to our earlier topic…*
As an aside, …	*OK, getting back on topic…*
That reminds me…	*So to return to what we were saying,…*
Signaling a Definition	**Talking about Visuals**
Which means…	*This graph/infographic/diagram shows/explains…*
What that means is…	*The line/box/image represents…*
Or…	*The main point of this visual is…*
In other words,…	*You can see…*
Another way to say that is…	*From this we can see…*
That is…	
That is to say…	

Conclusion	
Concluding	*To sum up,*
Well/So, that's how I see it.	*As you can see,…*
In conclusion,	*At the end,…*
In summary,	*To review, (+ restatement of main points)*

PRESENTATION STRATEGIES

You will often have to give individual or group presentations in your class. The strategies below will help you to prepare, present, and reflect on your presentations.

Prepare

As you prepare your presentation:

Consider Your Topic

- **Choose a topic you feel passionate about.** If you are passionate about your topic, your audience will be more interested and excited about your topic, too. Focus on one major idea that you can bring to life. The best ideas are the ones your audience wants to experience.

Consider Your Purpose

- **Have a strong start.** Use an effective hook, such as a quote, an interesting example, a rhetorical question, or a powerful image to get your audience's attention. Include one sentence that explains what you will do in your presentation and why.
- **Stay focused.** Make sure your details and examples support your main points. Avoid sidetracks or unnecessary information that takes you away from your topic.
- **Use visuals that relate to your ideas.** Drawings, photos, video clips, infographics, charts, maps, slides, and physical objects can get your audience's attention and explain ideas effectively. For example, a photo or map of a location you mention can help your audience picture a place they have never been. Slides with only key words and phrases can help emphasize your main points. Visuals should be bright, clear, and simple.
- **Have a strong conclusion.** A strong conclusion should serve the same purpose as a strong start—to get your audience's attention and make them think. Good conclusions often refer back to the introduction, or beginning of the presentation. For example, if you ask a question in the beginning, you can answer it in the conclusion. Remember to restate your main points, and add a conclusion device such as a question, a call to action, or a quote.

Consider your Audience

- **Use familiar concepts.** Think about the people in your audience. Ask yourself these questions: Where are they from? How old are they? What is their background? What do they already know about my topic? What information do I need to explain? Use language and concepts they will understand.
- **Share a personal story.** Consider presenting information that will get an emotional reaction; for example, information that will make your audience feel surprised, curious, worried, or upset. This will help your audience relate to you and your topic.
- **Be authentic (be yourself!).** Write your presentation yourself. Use words that you know and are comfortable using.

Rehearse

- **Make an outline** to help you organize your ideas.
- **Write notes on notecards.** Do not write full sentences, just key words and phrases to help you remember important ideas. Mark the words you should stress and places to pause.
- **Review pronunciation.** Check the pronunciation of words you are uncertain about with a classmate, a teacher, or in a dictionary. Note and practice the pronunciation of difficult words.
- **Memorize the introduction and conclusion.** Rehearse your presentation several times. Practice saying it out loud to yourself (perhaps in front of a mirror or video recorder) and in front of others.
- **Ask for feedback.** Note and revise information that doesn't flow smoothly based on feedback and on your own performance in rehearsal. If specific words or phrases are still a problem, rephrase them.

Present

As you present:

- **Pay attention to your pacing** (how fast or slow you speak). Remember to speak slowly and clearly. Pause to allow your audience to process information.
- **Speak at a volume loud enough to be heard** by everyone in the audience, but not too loud. Ask the audience if your volume is OK at the beginning of your talk.

- **Vary your intonation.** Don't speak in the same tone throughout the talk. Your audience will be more interested if your voice rises and falls, speeds up and slows down to match the ideas you are talking about.
- **Be friendly and relaxed with your audience**—remember to smile!
- **Show enthusiasm for your topic.** Use humor if appropriate.
- **Have a relaxed body posture.** Don't stand with your arms folded, or look down at your notes. Use gestures when helpful to emphasize your points.
- **Don't read directly from your notes.** Use them to help you remember ideas.
- **Don't look at or read from your visuals too much.** Use them to support your ideas.
- **Make frequent eye contact** with the entire audience.

Reflect

As you reflect on your presentation:

- **Consider what you think went well** during your presentation and what areas you can improve upon.
- **Get feedback** from your classmates and teacher. How do their comments relate to your own thoughts about your presentation? Did they notice things you didn't? How can you use their feedback in your next presentation?

PRESENTATION OUTLINE

When you are planning a presentation, you may find it helpful to use an outline. If it is a group presentation, the outline can provide an easy way to divide the content. For example, one student can do the introduction, another student the first idea in the body, and so on.

1. Introduction

Topic: _____

Hook: _____

Statement of main idea: _____

2. Body

First step/example/reason: _____

Supporting details: _____ _____ _____

Second step/example/reason: _____

Supporting details: _____ _____ _____

Third step/example/reason: _____

Supporting details: _____ _____ _____

3. Conclusion

Main points to summarize: _____ _____

Suggestions/Predictions: _____ _____

Closing comments/summary: _____ _____

PRONUNCIATION GUIDE

Sounds and Symbols

Vowels

Symbol	Key Words
/ɑ/	hot, stop
/æ/	cat, ran
/aɪ/	fine, nice
/i/	eat, need
/ɪ/	sit, him
/eɪ/	name, say
/ɛ/	get, bed
/ʌ/	cup, what
/ə/	about, lesson
/u/	boot, new
/ʊ/	book, could
/oʊ/	go, road
/ɔ/	law, walk
/aʊ/	house, now
/ɔɪ/	toy, coin

Consonants

Symbol	Key Word	Symbol	Key Word
/b/	boy	/t/	tea
/d/	day	/tʃ/	cheap
/dʒ/	job, bridge	/v/	vote
/f/	face	/w/	we
/g/	go	/y/	yes
/h/	hat	/z/	zoo
/k/	key, car		
/l/	love	/ð/	they
/m/	my	/θ/	think
/n/	nine	/ʃ/	shoe
/ŋ/	sing	/ʒ/	measure
/p/	pen		
/r/	right		
/s/	see		

Source: *The Newbury House Dictionary plus Grammar Reference,* Fifth Edition, National Geographic Learning/ Cengage Learning, 2014.

Rhythm

The rhythm of English involves stress and pausing.

Stress

- English words are based on syllables—units of sound that include one vowel sound.
- In every word in English, one syllable has the primary stress.
- In English, speakers group words that go together based on the meaning and context of the sentence. These groups of words are called *thought groups*. In each thought group, one word is stressed more than the others—the stress is placed on the syllable with the primary stress in this word.
- In general, new ideas and information are stressed.

Pausing

- Pauses in English can be divided into two groups: long and short pauses.
- English speakers use long pauses to mark the conclusion of a thought, items in a list, or choices given.
- Short pauses are used in between thought groups to break up the ideas in sentences into smaller, more manageable chunks of information.

English speakers use intonation, or pitch (the rise and fall of their voice), to help express meaning. For example, speakers usually use a rising intonation at the end of *yes/no* questions, and a falling intonation at the end of *wh-* questions and statements.

VOCABULARY BUILDING STRATEGIES

Vocabulary learning is an on-going process. The strategies below will help you learn and remember new vocabulary words.

Guessing Meaning from Context

You can often guess the meaning of an unfamiliar word by looking at or listening to the words and sentences around it. Speakers usually know when a word is unfamiliar to the audience, or is essential to understanding the main ideas, and often provide clues to its meaning.

- Repetition: A speaker may use the same key word or phrase, or use another form of the same word.
- Restatement or synonym: A speaker may give a synonym to explain the meaning of a word, using phrases such as, *in other words, also called, or…, also known as.*
- Antonyms: A speaker may define a word by explaining what it is NOT. The speaker may say *Unlike A/In contrast to A, B is…*
- Definition: Listen for signals such as *which means* or *is defined as.* Definitions can also be signaled by a pause.
- Examples: A speaker may provide examples that can help you figure out what something is. For example, ***Mascots*** *are a very popular marketing tool. You've seen them on commercials and in ads on social media –* **cute, brightly colored creatures that help sell a product***.*

Understanding Word Families: Stems, Prefixes, and Suffixes

Use your understanding of stems, prefixes, and suffixes to recognize unfamiliar words and to expand your vocabulary. The stem is the root part of the word, which provides the main meaning. A prefix comes before the stem and usually modifies meaning (e.g., adding *re-* to a word means "again" or "back"). A suffix comes after the stem and usually changes the part of speech (e.g., adding *-ion, -tion,* or *-ation* to a verb changes it to a noun). Words that share the same stem or root belong to the same word family (e.g., *event, eventful, uneventful, uneventfully*).

Word Stem	Meaning	Example
ann, enn	year	anniversary, millennium
chron(o)	time	chronological, synchronize
flex, flect	bend	flexible, reflection
graph	draw, write	graphics, paragraph
lab	work	labor, collaborate
mob, mot, mov	move	automobile, motivate, mover
port	carry	transport, import
sect	cut	sector, bisect

Prefix	Meaning	Example
dis-	not, opposite of	disappear, disadvantages
in-, im-, il-, ir-	not	inconsistent, immature, illegal, irresponsible
inter-	between	Internet, international
mis-	bad, badly, incorrectly	misunderstand, misjudge
pre-	before	prehistoric, preheat
re-	again; back	repeat; return
trans-	across, beyond	transfer, translate
un-	not	uncooked, unfair

Suffix	Meaning	Example
-able, -ible	worth, ability	believable, impossible
-en	to cause to become; made of	lengthen, strengthen; golden
-er, -or	one who	teacher, director
-ful	full of	beautiful, successful
-ify, -fy	to make or become	simplify, satisfy
-ion, -tion, -ation	condition, action	occasion, education, foundation
-ize	cause	modernize, summarize
-ly	in the manner of	carefully, happily
-ment	condition or result	assignment, statement
-ness	state of being	happiness, sadness

Using a Dictionary

Here are some tips for using a dictionary:

- When you see or hear a new word, try to guess its part of speech (noun, verb, adjective, etc.) and meaning, then look it up in a dictionary.

- Some words have multiple meanings. Look up a new word in the dictionary and try choose the correct meaning for the context. Then see if it makes sense within the context.

- When you look up a word, look at all the definitions to see if there is a basic core meaning. This will help you understand the word when it is used in a different context. Also look at all the related words, or words in the same family. This can help you expand your vocabulary. For example, the core meaning of *structure* involves something built or put together.

> **structure** / ˈstrʌktʃər/ *n.* **1** [C] a building of any kind: *A new structure is being built on the corner.* **2** [C] any architectural object of any kind: *The Eiffel Tower is a famous Parisian structure.* **3** [U] the way parts are put together or organized: *the structure of a song‖a business's structure*
> –*v.* [T] **-tured, -turing, -tures** to put together or organize parts of s.t.: *We are structuring a plan to hire new teachers.*
> –*adj.* **structural.**

Source: *The Newbury House Dictionary plus Grammar Reference*, Fifth Edition, National Geographic Learning/Cengage Learning, 2014

Multi-Word Units

You can improve your fluency if you learn and use vocabulary as multi-word units: idioms (*go the extra mile*), collocations (*wide range*), and fixed expressions (*in other words*). Some multi-word units can only be understood as a chunk – the individual words do not add up to the same overall meaning. Keep track of multi-word units in a notebook or on notecards.

Vocabulary Note Cards

You can expand your vocabulary by using vocabulary note cards or a vocabulary building app. Write the word, expression, or sentence that you want to learn on one side. On the other, draw a four-square grid and write the following information in the squares: definition; translation (in your first language); sample sentence; synonyms. Choose words that are high frequency or on the academic word list. If you have looked a word up a few times, you should make a card for it.

definition:	first language translation:
sample sentence:	synonyms:

Organize the cards in review sets so you can practice them. Don't put words that are similar in spelling or meaning in the same review set as you may get them mixed up. Go through the cards and test yourself on the words or expressions. You can also practice with a partner.

VOCABULARY INDEX

Word	Page	CEFR† Level	Word	Page	CEFR† Level
according to	14	B1	image	24	B2
achieve	54	B1	income	54	B2
active	14	B1	investigate	34	B2
affect*	14	B2	investor	44	B2
alive	34	B1	justify	14	B2
analyze/analyse*	34	B2	lead to	44	B2
ancient	24	B1	leave behind	14	B1
appreciate	54	B2	major*	4	B2
archaeologist	24	C1	material	4	B1
boundary	4	C1	mission	54	B2
bury	24	B1	motivation	44	B2
civilization/civilisation	24	B2	persistent	44	C2
collapse	4	B2	potential	54	B2
confidence	44	B2	precious	34	B2
considerable	54	B2	probability	54	C1
construct	4	B2	recognition	54	C2
definite	14	B2	reinforce	4	C1
determine	34	C1	remains	34	B1
dig	24	B1	report	34	B1
disaster	14	B2	reveal	24	B2
discovery	34	B2	royal	24	B2
earthquake	4	B2	ruins	24	B1
eruption	14	off list	rule	34	B1
essential	44	B1	shake	4	B1
evacuate	14	off list	soil	14	B2
eventually	44	B2	survive	4	B2
evidently*	54	B2	tomb	24	B2
evolve	44	C1	treasure	34	B2
failure	44	B2	uncertainty	44	C1
found	54	B2	zone	4	B1

†The Common European Framework of Reference for Languages (CEFR) is an international standard for describing language proficiency.

*These words are on the Academic Word List (AWL). The AWL is a list of the 570 highest-frequency academic word families that regularly appear in academic texts. The AWL was compiled by researcher Averil Coxhead based on her analysis of a 3.5-million-word corpus (Coxhead, 2000).

NOTES

NOTES

NOTES

NOTES

NOTES

NOTES